SPEECH ACTS

AN ESSAY IN THE
PHILOSOPHY OF LANGUAGE

SPEECH ACTS

AN ESSAY IN
THE PHILOSOPHY OF
LANGUAGE

JOHN R. SEARLE

Professor of Philosophy
University of California, Berkeley

CAMBRIDGE UNIVERSITY PRESS

CAMBRIDGE
LONDON   NEW YORK   NEW ROCHELLE
MELBOURNE   SYDNEY

Published by the Press Syndicate of the University of Cambridge
The Pitt Building, Trumpington Street, Cambridge CB2 1RP
32 East 57th Street, New York, NY 10022, USA
296 Beaconsfield Parade, Middle Park, Melbourne 3206, Australia

ISBN 0 521 07184 4 hard covers
ISBN 0 521 09626 X paperback

Library of Congress Catalog Card Number: 68–24484

First published 1969
Reprinted 1969, 1970, 1972,
1974, 1976, 1977, 1978, 1980

Printed in the United States of America
by the Murray Printing Co., Westford, Mass.

CONTENTS

v

Contents

PREFACE

In addition to its obvious debts to two of my teachers, J. L. Austin and P. F. Strawson, this book owes much to helpful advice and criticism from the many people who read and commented on portions of the manuscript: I am especially grateful to Julian Boyd, Noam Chomsky, R. M. Harnish, Benson Mates and Hans Sluga.

The nucleus of this work was my D.Phil. thesis on Sense and Reference submitted in Oxford in 1959. Several of the ideas presented here have appeared in articles by me, and I wish to thank the editors and publishers of *Mind*, *The Philosophical Review*, *The Encyclopedia of Philosophy* and Messrs Routledge & Kegan Paul and Allen & Unwin for permission to use some of this material again.

Thanks are also due to the American Council of Learned Societies for a grant which enabled me to work on these and related matters in 1963–4, Miss Ruth Anderson for supervising the typing, R. M. Harnish and M. Shapira for work on the index, D. Parfit for help with the proofs and R. B. Kitaj for designing the cover. Most of all I wish to thank my wife for continuing help and advice.

J. R. S.

FOR DAGMAR

PART ONE

A Theory of Speech Acts

NOTE

Excepting citation of articles, throughout this book double quotes are used for quotation and single quotes as 'scare quotes'.

Chapter 1

METHODS AND SCOPE

1.1 The philosophy of language

How do words relate to the world? How is it possible that when a speaker stands before a hearer and emits an acoustic blast such remarkable things occur as: the speaker means something; the sounds he emits mean something; the hearer understands what is meant; the speaker makes a statement, asks a question, or gives an order? How is it possible, for example, that when I say " Jones went home", which after all is in one way just a string of noises, what I mean is: Jones went home. What is the difference between saying something and meaning it and saying it without meaning it? And what is involved in meaning just one particular thing and not some other thing? For example, how does it happen that when people say, " Jones went home" they almost always mean Jones went home and not, say, Brown went to the party or Green got drunk. And what is the relation between what I mean when I say something and what it means whether anybody says it or not? How do words stand for things? What is the difference between a meaningful string of words and a meaningless one? What is it for something to be true? or false?

Such questions form the subject matter of the philosophy of language. We must not assume that in the versions I have stated they even make sense. Still, in some form or other some such questions must make sense; for we do know that people communicate, that they do say things and sometimes mean what they say, that they are, on occasion at least, understood, that they ask questions, issue orders, make promises, and give apologies, that people's utterances do relate to the world in ways we can describe by characterizing the utterances as being true or false or meaningless, stupid, exaggerated or what-not. And if these things do happen it follows that it is possible for them to happen, and if it is possible for them to happen it ought to be possible to pose and answer the questions which examine that possibility.

I distinguish between the philosophy of language and linguistic philosophy. Linguistic philosophy is the attempt to solve particular philosophical problems by attending to the ordinary use of particular words or other elements in a particular language. The philosophy of language is the attempt to give philosophically illuminating descriptions of certain general features of language, such as reference, truth, meaning, and necessity; and it is concerned only incidentally with particular elements in a particular language; though its method of investigation, where empirical and rational rather than *a priori* and speculative will naturally force it to pay strict attention to the facts of actual natural languages.

"Linguistic philosophy" is primarily the name of a method; "The philosophy of language" is the name of a subject. Although I shall sometimes employ the methods of linguistic philosophy, this book is an essay in the philosophy of language, not in linguistic philosophy.

It is not an essay in linguistics. Linguistics attempts to describe the actual structures—phonological, syntactical, and semantic—of natural human languages. The 'data' of the philosophy of language usually come from natural human languages, but many of the conclusions about e.g. what it is to be true or to be a statement or a promise, if valid, should hold for any possible language capable of producing truths or statements or promises. In that sense this essay is not in general about languages, French, English or Swahili, but is about language.

1.2 *Linguistic characterizations*

I shall approach the study of some of these problems in the philosophy of language through the study of what I call speech acts or linguistic acts or language acts. The reasons for adopting this approach will emerge later. In this section and the next I shall attempt to explain and justify the methods that I shall employ in conducting the investigation.

In the course of this work I shall make many remarks about language. Very roughly, most of these will fall into two types. First, I shall offer *characterizations* of linguistic elements. I shall say, for example, that such and such an expression is used to refer, or that such and such a combination of words makes no sense, or that such and such a proposition is analytic. Sometimes the characterizing term will be one I have invented. To have a name let us call such remarks *linguistic characterizations*. Secondly, I shall offer explanations of and generalizations from the facts recorded in linguistic characterizations. I shall say, for example, that we do not say such and such because there is a rule to the effect that so and so. Let us call such statements *linguistic explanations*. This distinction is not intended to be either razorsharp or airtight, but it will do for present purposes.

Now the question naturally arises how I know that what I have to say is true. Philosophers' puzzlement in this connection has tended to concentrate on linguistic characterizations and to take two forms: First, there has been a series of skeptical doubts about the criteria for the application of such terms as "analytic", "meaningful", "synonymous", and the like.[1] Secondly, there have been general doubts about the *verification* of statements about language.[2] These two forms of doubt are related; I shall consider them in order. Of the disputed characterizing terms, "analytic" and "synonymous" have received by far the most attention, and I shall begin by discussing them, though the form of the argument —on both sides—would apply to the others equally well.

It has often been suggested that we lack an adequate analysis of the concept of analyticity and consequently that we lack adequate criteria for deciding whether a statement is analytic. It is further suggested that because of this lack of analysis and criteria, we do not even properly understand the word and the very notion is illegitimate, defective, incoherent, unempirical, or the like. This form of argument—we lack analysis and criteria for a concept *C*, therefore we do not properly understand *C*, and until we can provide analysis and criteria for *C*, it is somehow or in some respects illegitimate—has frequently occurred in the writings of analytic philosophers since the war and it is worth examining in some detail.

First, it will not do to say simply that we lack criteria for analyticity or synonymy. In the (somewhat odd) sense of "criterion" which is employed in these discussions the definition that we could give for these terms provides a criterion of sorts.

[1] See for example W. Quine, 'Two dogmas of empiricism', *Philosophical Review*, January (1951), reprinted in W. Quine, *From a Logical Point of View* (Cambridge, 1961); and Morton White, 'The analytic and the synthetic, an untenable dualism', in L. Linsky, (ed.), *Semantics and the Philosophy of Language* (Urbana, 1952).

[2] See for example B. Mates, 'On the verification of statements about ordinary language', *Inquiry*, vol. 1 (1958); reprinted in V. C. Chappell (ed.), *Ordinary Language* (Englewood Cliffs, 1964).

Synonymy is defined as: two words are synonymous if and only if they have the same meaning; and analyticity is defined as: a statement is analytic if and only if it is true in virtue of its meaning or by definition. Such definitions are precisely the sort of thing one would give to someone who was seriously ignorant of what these words meant and wanted to know. No doubt, pedagogically speaking, they would need to be supplemented with examples in order to get our student to master the technique of using the words. But the criterion we have provided is quite clear: if you want to know if two words are synonymous ask yourself whether they mean the same. If you want to know if a statement is analytic ask yourself whether it is true by definition or in virtue of its meaning.

But, so the story goes, such definitions are no good because they rely on the notion of meaning and the notion of meaning is just as much unexplained, just as much in need of explication, as is the notion of synonymy or analyticity. What is wanted is a criterion of quite a different kind—extensional, formal, or behavioral; some way whereby, for example, by performing mechanical operations on sentences or observing the behavior of speakers one could decide whether or not a statement was analytic. A simple paraphrase in terms of equally puzzling notions will not do; what is wanted is some objective test for analyticity and synonymy. It is in absence of such a test that one finds these concepts defective.

In recent years various attempts have been made to meet such objections. I shall not try to meet the objections here, but will argue that the objections rest on certain general and mistaken assumptions about the relations between our understanding of a notion and our ability to provide criteria of a certain kind for its application.

To begin, let us provide a criterion of the proposed kind and see exactly why it is inadequate. Suppose we take as our criterion for analyticity the following: a statement is analytic if and only if the first word of the sentence used in making that statement begins with the letter "*A*". This criterion has all the formalist objectivity desired by the objectors to the notion of analyticity; but it is obviously absurd, as I think all the parties to the dispute would agree. Why exactly is it absurd? We all know it is absurd because we know that the first letter of the first word of a sentence used on a particular occasion to make a statement has nothing to do with the analyticity of the statement; and if pressed further for reasons we could provide an indefinite number of examples of analytic statements which do not begin with the letter "*A*" and an indefinite number of non-analytic statements which do begin with the letter "*A*". We could even go on to point out that the criterion would give the absurd result that the same statement could be both analytic and not analytic when stated in the utterance of different sentences (in different languages, for example). In short this criterion, like all other extensional criteria so far proposed for analyticity, will not do. But now, as we know the criterion to be inadequate and are able to give reasons for our claim that it is inadequate, the question naturally arises, how does this knowledge come about? How indeed do we even know that the reasons we give are even relevant to the problem? As an answer I wish to make and develop the following suggestion. We know these things precisely because we know what the word "analytic" means; further we could not know them if we did not know what "analytic" means. We know what sort of considerations influence the decision to characterize a statement as analytic or not and we know that spelling is not among them. But precisely that sort of knowledge is involved in knowing what the word means, and indeed is what constitutes knowing what it means. Far from showing that we do not understand the concept of analyticity, our failure to find criteria of the proposed kind presupposes precisely that we do understand analyticity. We could not embark on our investigation if we did not understand the concept, for it is only in virtue of that understanding that we could assess the adequacy of proposed criteria.

Any criterion for analyticity must be judged by its ability to give certain results. It must, for example, give the result that the statement "My son is now eating an apple" is not analytic, and "Rectangles are four-sided" is analytic. Anyone familiar with these terms is able to continue this list of examples indefinitely, and that ability is what constitutes an understanding of "analytic", indeed this ability is presupposed by a search for formal criteria for the explication of "analytic". I chose these two examples, "Rectangles are four-sided" and "My son is now eating an apple", because I have never seen either of them on a list of analytic or synthetic statements. I chose them to illustrate that our knowledge of the conditions of adequacy on proposed criteria for the concept analytic is of a *projective* kind. "Analytic" does not denote a closed class of statements; it is not an abbreviation for a list, but, as is characteristic of general terms, it has the possibility of projection. We know how to apply it to new cases.[1]

We test, then, any proposed criterion not merely on its ability to classify certain well worn examples (e.g., "All bachelors are unmarried") but by checking that its projective power is the same as "analytic", all of which, again, presupposes an understanding of the general term "analytic".

It is, therefore, a paradoxical feature of some of the attacks on the notions of synonymy and analyticity that the attacks should only have the force the authors intend them to have if it is presupposed that the notions of synonymy and analyticity are adequately understood. I shall illustrate this further. Quine says, attacking analyticity, "I do not know whether the statement "Everything green is extended" is analytic."[2] It is very revealing that this should be the example chosen. He does not say such things as, "I do not know whether "Oculists are eye doctors" is analytic", nor does he say, "I do not know whether "It is now raining" is analytic". That is, the example he has chosen is a borderline case. It is a borderline case because, for example, some people claim that there are such things as sense data, which can be green, but have denied that sense data can be spatially extended. The example has its effect precisely because it is a borderline case. We do not feel completely confident in classifying it either as analytic or non-analytic.[3] But our recognition of it as a puzzling case, far from showing that we do not have any adequate notion of analyticity, tends to show precisely the reverse. We could not recognize borderline cases of a concept as borderline cases if we did not grasp the concept to begin with. It is as much a test of a man's mastery of the concept *green* that he has doubts about applying it to a glass of Chartreuse, as that he has no doubt at all about applying it to a healthy lawn or withholding it from fresh snow. I, too, am unsure whether it is analytic that everything green is extended, which is evidence (though not more than just evidence), that I, too, understand the concept of analyticity quite well.

[1] For more on the importance of this projective quality, see P. Grice and P. F. Strawson, 'In defense of a dogma', *Philosophical Review* (April 1965).

[2] W. Quine, *op. cit.* p. 32.

[3] The point is not simply that it may not be *true*, as Grice and Strawson point out (*op. cit.* p. 153), but rather that it is not clear how we are to take it.

Another author[1] discussing synonymy once offered an analysis which has the consequence that no two words can be exactly synonymous.[2] Since, for example, the expression "eye doctor that is not an oculist" can be described as an eye doctor description but not as an oculist description, he argues that this shows there is something in the "secondary extension" of "eye doctor" which is not in that of "oculist".[3] And since a similar point can be made about any pair of words, he argues that no two different words can ever have "quite the same meaning".[4] But now let us reflect on what exactly is proven by such an argument. Is it not quite clear that what it shows is that such facts about secondary extensions have simply no bearing on whether two terms are synonymous? The starting point for any search for a criterion of synonymy is (and must be) such facts as that "oculist" means eye doctor. Any extensional criterion for a concept like synonymy would first have to be checked to make sure that it gave the right results, otherwise the choice of the criterion would be arbitrary and unjustified. The proposed criterion does not give the right results, nor is there any *a priori* reason why it should, and we must therefore abandon it.

The claim that "oculist" means eye doctor is not a claim that has to satisfy any criteria which philosophers might propose for synonymy, but rather any proposed criterion for synonymy has to be consistent with such facts as that "eye doctor" is synonymous with "oculist". Nor does the maneuver with the notion of

---

[1] N. Goodman, 'On likeness of meaning', *Analysis* (October 1949). A revised version appears in L. Linsky (ed.), *Semantics and the Philosophy of Language* (Urbana, 1952).

[2] Both Quine and Goodman seem to me to modify their positions in works subsequent to the two classic articles I have cited, and it is unlikely that they would hold exactly the same views today that they expounded in these articles. I am here concerned, however, not with the development of their thought as individual philosophers, but with a certain pattern of analysis in philosophy of which these two works are well-known and powerful examples.

Unfortunately some of the changes do not seem to be improvements. Quine offers a definition of "stimulus analyticity" as follows. "I call a sentence stimulus analytic for a subject if he would assent to it, or nothing, after every stimulus (within the modulus)" (*Word and Object*, Cambridge 1960, p. 55). Presumably then for most of us there would be no stimulus analytic sentences, because e.g. if the stimulus includes a gun at our head and the order, "Withhold assent from "All bachelors are unmarried" or I'll blow your brains out" it would take a hero to assent. Semantic information provides only one sort of motive among many for assenting to or witholding assent from utterances, and consequently dispositions to assent by themselves provide no basis for defining semantic notions.

[3] The pair of words chosen is my example, but illustrates his argument.

[4] Linsky (ed.), *op. cit.* p. 74.

exactness offer any help; for, as Wittgenstein[1] pointed out, exactness is relative to some purpose; and relative to the purposes for which we employ synonyms, "oculist" is exactly synonymous with "eye doctor". For example, my child, who knows the meaning of "eye doctor" but not of "oculist", asks me, "What does oculist mean?" I tell him, ""Oculist" means eye doctor." Have I not told him exactly what he wanted to know?

I think in fact that the notions of analyticity and synonymy are not very useful philosophical tools. There are too many borderline cases and too few clear cut examples. In the case of analyticity, there are too many kinds of propositions included within the denotation and too many unanswered questions (e.g., are arithmetical statements really enough like the paradigms of analyticity to be called "analytic"?) for the term to be other than a very blunt tool of philosophical analysis. But, again, the very discovery of its bluntness and the consequent misgivings about its usefulness presuppose a grasp of the concept and of the distinction between analytic and non-analytic propositions.

In sum, the form of argument which takes a concept which is in usage and about which there is general agreement—of a projective kind—about its applicability and says of that concept that it is somehow defective, because there are no criteria of a certain kind for its applicability, could never by itself establish that the concept was not understood or was invalid. The most the argument could show is that it is inappropriate to ask for criteria of the proposed kind.

The tacit ideology which seems to lie behind these objections is that non-extensional explications are not explications at all and that any concept which is not extensionally explicable is defective. My argument is that the form of the argument is self-defeating. You could not know that a given extensional criterion failed without having some conception of what constituted success or failure. But to have that is in general to understand the concept.

I am not, of course, saying that it is impossible in any way to show that the use of a concept concerning which there is projective agreement is defective. For example, a tribe might agree on who is and who is not a witch, but one could still show that their talk was muddled and unempirical in various ways. But think how one would actually have to go about it. One would,

---

[1] Ludwig Wittgenstein, *Philosophical Investigation* (New York, 1953), para. 88.

for example, have to find out what they meant by "witch" and then show that the actual tests they used to determine who was a witch, e.g., being an old woman accused by certain informers of being a witch, could never prove that anybody was actually a witch, i.e., had the various super-natural powers included in the meaning of "witch".

Similarly, one sometimes explains to someone that a proposition he thought was analytic is really not analytic or that a pair of expressions he thought were synonymous are not in fact so. But, again, think of how one actually goes about it. For example, when a beginning philosophy student says, ""*X* is good" means"I like *X*"", to show him that he is mistaken, one adduces examples of things that one likes but would not say were good or shows that certain forms of words make a kind of sense they could not make if "*X* is good" just meant "I like *X*", such as e.g. "I like it, but is it really any good?" The intellectual underpinnings of such discussions will be examined in the next section.

As a native speaker of English I know that "oculist" is exactly synonymous with "eye doctor", that "bank" has (at least) two meanings, that "cat" is a noun, that "oxygen" is unambiguous, that "Shakespeare was a better playwright than poet" is meaningful, that "the slithy toves did gyre" is nonsensical, that "The cat is on the mat" is a sentence, etc. Yet I have no operational criteria for synonymy, ambiguity, nounhood, meaningfulness, or sentence-hood. Furthermore, any criterion for any one of these concepts has to be consistent with my (our) knowledge or must be abandoned as inadequate. The starting point, then, for this study is that one knows such facts about language independently of any ability to provide criteria of the preferred kinds for such knowledge.

Any appeal to a criterion presupposes the adequacy of the criterion and that adequacy can only be established by testing the criterion against examples such as these. The point is not that the claims made in linguistic characterizations cannot be justified in the absence of the preferred kinds of criteria, but rather that any proposed criterion cannot be justified in the absence of antecedent knowledge expressed by linguistic characterizations.

I do not, of course, intend these remarks to belittle the search for criteria as an enterprise. Indeed, I think—properly construed —such attempts to find criteria for our concepts are in fact attempts to explicate our concepts, which I take to be one of the central tasks of philosophy. My only point at present is that where certain preferred models of explication fail to account for certain concepts it is the models which must go, not the concepts.

1.3   *The 'verification' of linguistic characterizations*

What I have said so far raises the prior question: How do I know the sorts of things about language that I claim to know? Even assuming that I do not need to back my intuitions by appeal to criteria of certain sorts, still if they are to be shown to be valid must they not be backed by something? What sorts of explanation, or account, or justification could I offer for the claim that such and such a string of words is a sentence or that "oculist" means eye doctor or that it is analytically true that women are females? How, in short, are such claims to be verified? These questions acquire a particular urgency if they are taken as expressions of the following underlying question: "Is it not the case that all such knowledge, if really valid, must be based on an empirical scrutiny of human linguistic behavior?" How could one know such things unless one had done a really exhaustive statistical survey of the verbal behavior of English speakers and thus discovered how they in fact used words? Pending such a survey, is not all such talk mere prescientific speculation?

As a step toward answering these challenges, I wish to make and develop the following suggestion. Speaking a language is engaging in a (highly complex) rule-governed form of behavior. To learn and master a language is (*inter alia*) to learn and to have mastered these rules. This is a familiar view in philosophy and linguistics, but its consequences are not always fully realized. Its consequence, for the present discussion, is that when I, speaking as a native speaker, make linguistic characterizations of the kind exemplified above, I am not reporting the behavior of a group but describing aspects of my mastery of a rule-governed skill. And— this is also important—since the linguistic characterizations, if made in the same language as the elements characterized, are themselves utterances in accordance with the rules, such characterizations are manifestations of that mastery.[1]

---

[1] Of course, there are other kinds of linguistic characterizations for which this description would not hold, e.g., "the average American utters 2432 words a day". This is an empirical generalization concerning the verbal behavior of a group. I am not now concerned with such kinds of linguistic characterization.

By reflecting on linguistic elements I can offer linguistic characterizations which do not record particular utterances but have a general character, deriving from the fact that the elements are governed by rules. The 'justification' I have for my linguistic intuitions as expressed in my linguistic characterizations is simply that I am a native speaker of a certain dialect of English and consequently have mastered the rules of that dialect, which mastery is both partially described by and manifested in my linguistic characterizations of elements of that dialect. The only answer that I can give to the question, how do you know? (e.g., that "Women are female" is analytic), is to give other linguistic characterizations ("woman" means adult human female) or, if pushed by the insistent how-do-you-know question beyond linguistic characterizations altogether, to say "I speak English".

It is possible (equals not self contradictory) that other people in what I suppose to be my dialect group have internalized different rules and consequently my linguistic characterizations would not match theirs. But it is not possible that my linguistic characterizations of my own speech, of the kind exemplified above, are false statistical generalizations from insufficient empirical data, for they are not statistical, nor other kinds of empirical generalizations, at all. That my idiolect matches a given dialect group is indeed an empirical hypothesis (for which I have a lifetime of 'evidence'), but the truth that in my idiolect "oculist" means eye doctor is not refuted by evidence concerning the behavior of others (though, if I find that my rules do not match those of others, I shall alter my rules to conform). In short, the possibility of my coming to know and being able to state such facts as are recorded in linguistic characterizations of the kind we have been considering without following certain orthodox paradigms of empirical verification · is to be explained by the following. My knowledge of how to speak the language involves a mastery of a system of rules which renders my use of the elements of that language regular and systematic. By reflecting on my use of the elements of the language I can come to know the facts recorded in linguistic characterizations. And those characterizations can have a generality which goes beyond this or that instance of the use of the elements in question, even though the characterizations are not based on a large or even statistically interesting sample of the occurrences of the elements, because the rules guarantee generality.

An analogy: I know that in baseball after hitting the ball fair, the batter runs in the direction of first base, and not in the direction, say, of third base or the left field grand stand. Now what sort of knowledge is this? On what is it based? How is it possible? Notice that it is a general claim and not confined to this or that instance of baserunning behavior. I have never done or even seen a study of baserunner behavior, and I have never looked the matter up in a book. Furthermore, I know that if the book, even if it were a rule book, said anything to the contrary it would be mistaken or describing a different game or some such. My knowledge is based on knowing how to play baseball, which is *inter alia* having internalized a set of rules. I wish to suggest that my knowledge of linguistic characterizations is of a similar kind.

If this is correct, then the answer to the philosopher's question, "What would we say if...?" is not a prediction about future verbal behavior but a hypothetical statement of intention within a system of rules, where mastery of the rules dictates the answer (provided, of course, that both the rules and the question are determinate enough to dictate an answer, conditions which are by no means always satisfied).

On this account there is nothing infallible about linguistic characterizations; speakers' intuitions are notoriously fallible. It is not always easy to characterize one's skills and the fact that in these cases the skill is involved in giving the characterization does not serve to simplify matters.[1] There is also the general difficulty in correctly formulating knowledge that one has prior to and independent of any formulation; of converting *knowing how* into *knowing that*. We all know in one important sense what "cause" "intend", and "mean" mean, but it is not easy to *state* exactly what they mean. The mistakes we make and the mistakes I shall make in linguistic characterizations in the course of this work will be due to such things as not considering enough examples or mis-describing the examples considered, not to mention carelessness, insensitivity, and obtuseness; but, to repeat, they will not be due to over-hasty generalization from insufficient empirical data concerning the verbal behavior of groups, for there will be no such generalization nor such data.

We need to distinguish between (*a*) talking, (*b*) characterizing talk,

[1] A similar point is made in a slightly different context by Noam Chomsky, *Aspects of the Theory of Syntax* (Cambridge, 1965), pp. 21–4.

and (*c*) explaining talk—the difference between e.g., (*a*) "That's an apple", (*b*) ""Apple" is a noun", and (*c*) "The rule for the indefinite article preceding a noun beginning with a vowel requires an "n" as in "an apple"". (*b*) and (*c*) are linguistic characterizations and explanations respectively. I have been emphasizing that the ability to do (*a*) is what underlies and, indeed, what explains the possibility of knowledge of certain kinds of statements of kind (*b*). It is the data of kind (*a*) as recorded in statements of kind (*b*) which are explained by explanations of kind (*c*). The philosophical controversies over (*b*) statements have prompted me to this discussion of their epistemological status. But (*c*) statements have raised no such controversial dust, and I shall say nothing about them save that they are subject to the usual (vaguely expressed and difficult to explicate) constraints on any explanation whether in the exact sciences or elsewhere. Like all explanations, to be any good, they must account for the data, they must not be inconsistent with other data, and they must have such other vaguely defined features as simplicity, generality, and testability.

So, in our era of extremely sophisticated methodologies, the methodology of this book must seem naively simple. I am a native speaker of a language. I wish to offer certain characterizations and explanations of my use of elements of that language. The hypothesis on which I am proceeding is that my use of linguistic elements is underlain by certain rules. I shall therefore offer linguistic characterizations and then explain the data in those characterizations by formulating the underlying rules.

This method, as I have been emphasizing, places a heavy reliance on the intuitions of the native speaker. But everything I have ever read in the philosophy of language, even work by the most behavioristic and empirical of authors, relies similarly on the intuitions of the speaker. Indeed, it is hard to see how it could be otherwise since a serious demand that I justify my intuitions that "bachelor" means unmarried man, if consistent, would also involve the demand that I justify my intuition that a given occurrence of "bachelor" means the same as another occurrence of "bachelor". Such intuitions can indeed be justified, but only by falling back on other intuitions.

1.4 *Why study speech acts?*

I said in the last section that I hypothesize that speaking a language is engaging in a rule-governed form of behavior. I did not attempt to prove that hypothesis, rather I offered it by way of explanation of the fact that the sort of knowledge expressed in linguistic characterizations of the kind exemplified is possible. In a sense this entire book might be construed as an attempt to explore, to spell out some of the implications of, and so to test that hypothesis. There is nothing circular in this procedure, for I am using the hypothesis of language as rule-governed intentional behavior to explain the possibility of, not to provide evidence for, linguistic characterizations. The form that this hypothesis will take is that speaking a language is performing speech acts, acts such as making statements, giving commands, asking questions, making promises, and so on; and more abstractly, acts such as referring and pre-dicating; and, secondly, that these acts are in general made possible by and are performed in accordance with certain rules for the use of linguistic elements.

The reason for concentrating on the study of speech acts is simply this: all linguistic communication involves linguistic acts. The unit of linguistic communication is not, as has generally been supposed, the symbol, word or sentence, or even the token of the symbol, word or sentence, but rather the production or issuance of the symbol or word or sentence in the performance of the speech act. To take the token as a message is to take it as a produced or issued token. More precisely, the production or issuance of a sentence token under certain conditions is a speech act, and speech acts (of certain kinds to be explained later) are the basic or minimal units of linguistic communication. A way to come to see this point is to ask oneself, what is the difference between regarding an object as an instance of linguistic communication and not so regarding it? One crucial difference is this. When I take a noise or a mark on a piece of paper to be an instance of linguistic com-munication, as a message, one of the things I must assume is that the noise or mark was produced by a being or beings more or less like myself and produced with certain kinds of intentions. If I regard the noise or mark as a natural phenomenon like the wind in the trees or a stain on the paper, I exclude it from the class of linguistic communication, even though the noise or mark may be indistinguishable from spoken or written words. Furthermore, not only must I assume the noise or mark to have been produced as a result of intentional behavior, but I must also assume that the intentions are of a very special kind peculiar to speech acts. For example, it would be possible to communicate by arranging items of furniture in certain ways. The attitude one would have to such an arrangement of furniture, if one 'understood' it, would be quite different from the attitude I have, say, to the arrangement of furniture in this room, even though in both cases I might regard the arrangement as resulting from intentional behavior. Only certain kinds of intentions are adequate for the behavior I am calling speech acts. (These kinds of intentions will be explored in chapter 2.)

It might be objected to this approach that such a study deals only with the point of intersection of a theory of language and a theory of action. But my reply to that would be that if my conception of language is correct, a theory of language is part of a theory of action, simply because speaking is a rule-governed form of behavior. Now, being rule-governed, it has formal features which admit of independent study. But a study purely of those formal features, without a study of their role in speech acts, would be like a formal study of the currency and credit systems of economies without a study of the role of currency and credit in economic transactions. A great deal can be said in the study of language without studying speech acts, but any such purely formal theory is necessarily incomplete. It would be as if baseball were studied only as a formal system of rules and not as a game.

It still might seem that my approach is simply, in Saussurian terms, a study of "parole" rather than "langue". I am arguing, however, that an adequate study of speech acts is a study of *langue*. There is an important reason why this is true which goes beyond the claim that communication necessarily involves speech acts. I take it to be an analytic truth about language that whatever can be meant can be said. A given language may not have a syntax or a vocabulary rich enough for me to say what I mean in that language but there are no barriers in principle to supplementing the impoverished language or saying what I mean in a richer one.

There are, therefore, not two irreducibly distinct semantic studies, one a study of the meanings of sentences and one a study of the performances of speech acts. For just as it is part of our notion of the meaning of a sentence that a literal utterance of that sentence with that meaning in a certain context would be the performance of a particular speech act, so it is part of our notion of a speech act that there is a possible sentence (or sentences) the utterance of which in a certain context would in virtue of its (or their) meaning constitute a performance of that speech act.

The speech act or acts performed in the utterance of a sentence are in general a function of the meaning of the sentence. The meaning of a sentence does not in all cases uniquely determine what speech act is performed in a given utterance of that sentence, for a speaker may mean more than what he actually says, but it is always in principle possible for him to say exactly what he means. Therefore, it is in principle possible for every speech act one performs or could perform to be uniquely determined by a given sentence (or set of sentences), given the assumptions that the speaker is speaking literally and that the context is appropriate. And for these reasons a study of the meaning of sentences is not in principle distinct from a study of speech acts. Properly construed, they are the same study. Since every meaningful sentence in virtue of its meaning can be used to perform a particular speech act (or range of speech acts), and since every possible speech act can in principle be given an exact formulation in a sentence or sentences (assuming an appropriate context of utterance), the study of the meanings of sentences and the study of speech acts are not two independent studies but one study from two different points of view.

It is possible to distinguish at least two strands in contemporary work in the philosophy of language—one which concentrates on the uses of expressions in speech situations and one which concentrates on the meaning of sentences. Practitioners of these two approaches sometimes talk as if they were inconsistent, and at least some encouragement is given to the view that they are inconsistent by the fact that historically they have been associated with inconsistent views about meaning. Thus, for example, Wittgenstein's early work, which falls within the second strand, contains views about meaning which are rejected in his later work, which falls within the first strand. But although historically there have been sharp disagreements between practitioners of these two approaches, it is important to realize that the two approaches, construed not as theories but as approaches to investigation, are complementary and not competing. A typical question in the second approach is, "How do the meanings of the elements of a sentence determine the meaning of the whole sentence?"[1] A typical question in the first approach is, "What are the different kinds of speech acts speakers perform when they utter expressions?"[2] Answers to both questions are necessary to a complete philosophy of language, and more importantly, the two questions are necessarily related. They are related because for every possible speech act there is a possible sentence or set of sentences the literal utterance of which in a particular context would constitute a performance of that speech act.

1.5   *The principle of expressibility*

The principle that whatever can be meant can be said, which I shall refer to as the "principle of expressibility", is important for the subsequent argument of this book and I shall expand on it briefly, especially since it is possible to misconstrue it in ways which would render it false.

Often we mean more than we actually say. If you ask me "Are you going to the movies?" I may respond by saying "Yes" but, as is clear from the context, what I mean is "Yes, I am going to the movies", not "Yes, it is a fine day" or "Yes, we have no bananas". Similarly, I might say "I'll come" and mean it as a promise to come, i.e., mean it as I would mean "I promise that I will come", if I were uttering that sentence and meaning literally what I say. In such cases, even though I do not say exactly what I mean, it is always possible for me to do so—if there is any possibility that the hearer might not understand me, I may do so. But often I am unable to say exactly what I mean even if I want to because I do not know the language well enough to say what I mean (if I am speaking Spanish, say), or worse yet, because the language may not contain words or other devices for saying what I mean. But even in cases where it is in fact impossible to say exactly what I mean it is in principle possible to come to be able to say exactly what I mean. I can in principle if not in fact increase my knowledge of the language, or more radically, if the existing language or existing languages are not adequate to the task, if they simply

---

[1] Cf. J. Katz, *The Philosophy of Language* (New York, 1966).
[2] Cf. J. L. Austin, *How to Do Things with Words* (Oxford, 1962).

lack the resources for saying what I mean, I can in principle at least enrich the language by introducing new terms or other devices into it. Any language provides us with a finite set of words and syntactical forms for saying what we mean, but where there is in a given language or in any language an upper bound on the expressible, where there are thoughts that cannot be expressed in a given language or in any language, it is a contingent fact and not a necessary truth.

We might express this principle by saying that for any meaning X and any speaker S whenever S means (intends to convey, wishes to communicate in an utterance, etc.) X then it is possible that there is some expression E such that E is an exact expression of or formulation of X. Symbolically: $(S)(X)(S$ means $X \rightarrow P(\exists E)$ (E is an exact expression of X)).[1]

To avoid two sorts of misunderstandings, it should be emphasized that the principle of expressibility does not imply that it is always possible to find or invent a form of expression that will produce all the effects in hearers that one means to produce; for example, literary or poetic effects, emotions, beliefs, and so on. We need to distinguish what a speaker means from certain kinds of effects he intends to produce in his hearers. This topic will be expanded in chapter 2. Secondly, the principle that whatever can be meant can be said does not imply that whatever can be said can be understood by others; for that would exclude the possibility of a private language, a language that it was logically impossible for anyone but the speaker to understand. Such languages may indeed be logically impossible, but I shall not attempt to decide that question in the course of the present investigation.

This principle has wide consequences and ramifications. It will, e.g. (in chapter 4), enable us to account for important features of Frege's theory of sense and reference. It has the consequence that cases where the speaker does not say exactly what he means—the principal kinds of cases of which are nonliteralness, vagueness, ambiguity, and incompleteness—are not theoretically essential to linguistic communication. But most important for present purposes it enables us to equate rules for performing speech acts with rules for uttering certain linguistic elements, since for any possible

[1] This formulation involves an explicit use of quantifiers through a modal context; but since the kind of entity quantified over is 'intensional' anyway, the modal context does not seem to raise any special problems.

speech act there is a possible linguistic element the meaning of which (given the context of the utterance) is sufficient to determine that its literal utterance is a performance of precisely that speech act. To study the speech acts of promising or apologizing we need only study sentences whose literal and correct utterance would constitute making a promise or issuing an apology.

The hypothesis that the speech act is the basic unit of communication, taken together with the principle of expressibility, suggests that there are a series of analytic connections between the notion of speech acts, what the speaker means, what the sentence (or other linguistic element) uttered means, what the speaker intends, what the hearer understands, and what the rules governing the linguistic elements are. The aim of the next four chapters is to explore some of those connections.

Chapter 2

EXPRESSIONS, MEANING AND SPEECH ACTS

The hypothesis then of this work is that speaking a language is engaging in a rule-governed form of behavior. To put it more briskly, talking is performing acts according to rules. In order to substantiate that hypothesis and explicate speech, I shall state some of the rules according to which we talk. The procedure which I shall follow is to state a set of necessary and sufficient conditions for the performance of particular kinds of speech acts and then extract from those conditions sets of semantic rules for the use of the linguistic devices which mark the utterances as speech acts of those kinds. That is a rather bigger task than perhaps it sounds, and this chapter will be devoted to preparing the ground for it by introducing distinctions between *different kinds of speech acts*, and discussing the notions of *propositions, rules, meaning, and facts*.

2.1 *Expressions and kinds of speech acts*

Let us begin this phase of our inquiry by making some distinctions which naturally suggest themselves to us as soon as we begin to reflect on simple speech situations. (The simplicity of the sentences in our examples will not detract from the generality of the distinctions we are trying to make.) Imagine a speaker and a hearer and suppose that in appropriate circumstances the speaker utters one of the following sentences:

1. Sam smokes habitually.
2. Does Sam smoke habitually?
3. Sam, smoke habitually!
4. Would that Sam smoked habitually.

Now let us ask how we might characterize or describe the speaker's utterance of one of these. What shall we say the speaker is doing when he utters one of these?
One thing is obvious: anyone who utters one of these can be

said to have uttered a sentence formed of words in the English language. But clearly this is only the beginning of a description, for the speaker in uttering one of these is characteristically saying something and not merely mouthing words. In uttering 1 a speaker is making (what philosophers call) an assertion, in 2 asking a question, in 3 giving an order, and in 4 (a somewhat archaic form) expressing a wish or desire. And in the performance of each of these four different acts the speaker performs certain other acts which are common to all four: in uttering any of these the speaker *refers to* or mentions or designates a certain object Sam, and he predicates the expression "smokes habitually" (or one of its inflections) of the object referred to. Thus we shall say that in the utterance of all four the reference and predication are the same, though in each case the same reference and predication occur as part of a complete speech act which is different from any of the other three. We thus detach the notions of referring and predicating from the notions of such complete speech acts as asserting, questioning, commanding, etc., and the justification for this separation lies in the fact that the same reference and predication can occur in the performance of different complete speech acts. Austin baptized these complete speech acts with the name "illocutionary acts", and I shall henceforth employ this terminology.[1] Some of the English verbs denoting illocutionary acts are "state", "describe", "assert", "warn", "remark", "comment", "command", "order", "request", "criticize", "apologize", "censure", "approve", "welcome", "promise", "object", "demand", and "argue". Austin claimed there were over a thousand such expressions in English.[2]

The first upshot of our preliminary reflections, then, is that in the utterance of any of the four sentences in the example a speaker is characteristically performing at least three distinct kinds of acts. (*a*) The uttering of words (morphemes, sentences); (*b*) referring and predicating; (*c*) stating, questioning, commanding, promising, etc.

Let us assign names to these under the general heading of speech acts:

---

[1] J. L. Austin, *How to Do Things with Words* (Oxford, 1962). I employ the expression, "illocutionary act", with some misgivings, since I do not accept Austin's distinction between *locutionary* and *illocutionary* acts. Cf. J. R. Searle, 'Austin on Locutionary and Illocutionary Acts', *Philosophical Review*, forthcoming.

[2] Austin, *op. cit.* p. 149.

(*a*) Uttering words (morphemes, sentences) = performing *utterance acts*.

(*b*) Referring and predicating = performing *propositional acts*.

(*c*) Stating, questioning, commanding, promising, etc. = performing *illocutionary acts*.

I am not saying, of course, that these are separate things that speakers do, as it happens, simultaneously, as one might smoke, read and scratch one's head simultaneously, but rather that in performing an illocutionary act one characteristically performs propositional acts and utterance acts. Nor should it be thought from this that utterance acts and propositional acts stand to illocutionary acts in the way buying a ticket and getting on a train stand to taking a railroad trip. They are not means to ends; rather, utterance acts stand to propositional and illocutionary acts in the way in which, e.g., making an "X" on a ballot paper stands to voting.

The point of abstracting each of these kinds is that the 'identity criteria' are different in each case. We have already seen that the same propositional acts can be common to different illocutionary acts, and it is obvious that one can perform an utterance act without performing a propositional or illocutionary act at all. (One can utter words without saying anything.) And similarly, if we consider the utterance of a sentence such as:

5. Mr Samuel Martin is a regular smoker of tobacco

we can see reasons for saying that in certain contexts a speaker in uttering it would be performing the same propositional act as in 1–4 (reference and predication would be the same), the same illocutionary act as 1 (same statement or assertion is made), but a different utterance act from any of the first four since a different sentence, containing none of the same words and only some of the same morphemes, is uttered. Thus, in performing different utterance acts, a speaker may perform the same propositional and illocutionary acts. Nor, of course, need the performance of the same utterance act by two different speakers, or by the same speaker on different occasions, be a performance of the same propositional and illocutionary acts: the same sentence may, e.g., be used to make two different statements. Utterance acts consist simply in uttering strings of words. Illocutionary and propositional acts consist characteristically in uttering words in sentences in certain contexts, under certain conditions and with certain intentions, as we shall see later on.

So far I make no claims for dividing things up this way, other than its being a permissible way to divide them—vague though this may be. In particular, I do not claim that it is the only way to divide things. For example, for certain purposes one might wish to break up what I have called utterance acts into phonetic acts, phonemic acts, morphemic acts, etc. And, of course, for most purposes, in the science of linguistics it is not necessary to speak of acts at all. One can just discuss phonemes, morphemes, sentences, etc.

To these three notions I now wish to add Austin's notion of the *perlocutionary act*. Correlated with the notion of illocutionary acts is the notion of the consequences or *effects* such acts have on the actions, thoughts, or beliefs, etc. of hearers. For example, by arguing I may *persuade* or *convince* someone, by warning him I may *scare* or *alarm* him, by making a request I may *get him to do something*, by informing him I may *convince him* (*enlighten, edify, inspire him, get him to realize*). The italicized expressions above denote perlocutionary acts.

Correlative with the notion of propositional acts and illocutionary acts, respectively, are certain kinds of expressions uttered in their performance: the characteristic grammatical form of the illocutionary act is the complete sentence (it can be a one-word sentence); and the characteristic grammatical form of the propositional acts are parts of sentences: grammatical predicates for the act of predication, and proper names, pronouns, and certain other sorts of noun phrases for reference. Propositional acts cannot occur alone; that is, one cannot *just* refer and predicate without making an assertion or asking a question or performing some other illocutionary act. The linguistic correlate of this point is that sentences, not words, are used to say things. This is also what Frege meant when he said that only in the context of a sentence do words have reference—"Nur im Zusammenhang eines Satzes bedeuten die Wörter etwas."[1] The same thing in my terminology: One only refers as part of the performance of an illocutionary act, and the grammatical clothing of an illocutionary act is the complete sentence. An utterance of a referring expression only counts as referring if one says something.

[1] G. Frege, *Die Grundlagen der Arithmetik* (Breslau, 1884), p. 73.

The parallel between kinds of expressions and propositional acts is not, of course, exact. If I say, e.g., " He left me in the lurch", I am not referring to a particular lurch in which I was left, though phrases of the form "the so-and-so" are characteristically referring expressions.

2.2   *Predication*

My use of the verb "predicate" departs seriously from the traditional philosophic use and requires justification. First, expressions, not universals, are predicated of objects.[1] I adopt this convention because the introduction of universals seems to me both misleading and unnecessary in giving an account of the use of predicate expressions (cf. chapter 5), and also because I wish to bring out the connection between the notion of predication and the notion of truth: expressions, not universals, can be said to be true or false of objects. Secondly, in my terminology the same predication is said to occur in 1–5, whereas most philosophers speak as though predication only occurred in assertions, and hence no predication would occur in the utterance of 2–4. This seems to me not merely an inconvenient terminology—failing to allow us to mark the use of inflections of a common predicate expression in different kinds of illocutionary acts—but it also shows a profound miscomprehension of the similarity between assertions and other illocutionary acts, and the distinction of all illocutionary acts from propositions, a distinction which I shall shortly elucidate (in section 2.4).

2.3   *Reference as a speech act*

I shall now attempt partially to clarify the notion of referring. Examples of what I shall call singular definite referring expressions ("referring expressions" for short) are such expressions as "you", "the battle of Waterloo", "our copy of yesterday's newspaper", "Caesar", "the constellation of Orion". It is characteristic of each of these expressions that their utterance serves to pick out or identify one 'object' or 'entity' or 'particular' apart from other objects, about which the speaker then goes on to say something, or ask some question, etc. Any expression which serves to identify

---

[1] But identity of the expression predicated is not a necessary condition of identity of predication. Different but synonymous expressions can be used to make the same predication, e.g., "is an habitual smoker" and "smokes habitually".

any thing, process, event, action, or any other kind of 'individual' or 'particular' I shall call a referring expression. Referring expressions point to particular things; they answer the questions "Who?" "What?" "Which?" It is by their function, not always by their surface grammatical form or their manner of performing their function, that referring expressions are to be known.

These remarks perhaps will be a bit clearer if we contrast paradigm singular definite referring expressions with certain other kinds of expressions. Expressions beginning with the indefinite article, such as "a man", as it occurs in the utterance of the sentence, "A man came", might be said to refer to a particular man,[1] but they do not serve to identify or to indicate the speaker's intention to identify an object in the manner of some uses of expressions with the definite article, such as "the man". We need, therefore, to distinguish between singular definite referring expressions and singular indefinite referring expressions. Similarly we will need to distinguish between plural definite referring expressions (e.g., "the men") and plural indefinite referring expressions (e.g., "some men" as in "Some men came").

We must also distinguish referring from non-referring uses of expressions formed with the indefinite article: e.g., the occurrence of "a man" in the utterance of "A man came" is to be distinguished from its occurrence in the utterance of "John is a man". The first is referential, the second predicative. Russell[2] once held that these are both referring uses and that the second sentence is used to make an identity statement. This is obviously false, since if the second were an identity statement, then in the negative form "John is not a man", it would make sense to ask which man is it that John is not, which is absurd.

We might also distinguish those expressions which are used to refer to individuals or particulars from those which are used to refer to what philosophers have called universals: e.g., to distinguish such expressions as "Everest" and "this chair" from "the number three", "the color red" and "drunkenness". Unless otherwise indicated, I shall confine the terms "referring expressions" to expressions used to refer to particulars and postpone

[1] There is a case for refusing to call such utterances instances of *reference* at all. I do not discuss the problem, as my present purpose is only to contrast singular definite referring expressions with other kinds of expressions.

[2] B. Russell, *Introduction to Mathematical Philosophy* (London, 1919), p. 172.

my discussion of reference to universals until chapter 5. I shall use the term "referring expression" as short for "singular definite expression used for referring to particulars." The term "referring expression" is not meant to imply that expressions refer. On the contrary, as previously emphasized, reference is a speech act, and speech acts are performed by speakers in uttering words, not by words. To say that an expression refers (predicates, asserts, etc.) in my terminology is either senseless or is shorthand for saying that the expression is used by speakers to refer (predicate, assert, etc.); this is a shorthand I shall frequently employ.

The notion of definite reference and the cognate notion of definite referring expression lack precise boundaries. One can give a set of sentences containing such expressions to illustrate the paradigm cases of definite reference, but there will still be many cases where one is in doubt whether or not to describe the use of a word as an instance of reference. In signing one's name to a document does one *refer* to oneself? Do tensed verbs *refer* to the time of their utterance? These instances seem to lack many of the features which give *point* to paradigm definite references. A common mistake in philosophy is to suppose there must be a right and unequivocal answer to such questions, or worse yet, to suppose that unless there is a right and unequivocal answer, the concept of referring is a worthless concept. The proper approach, I suggest, is to examine those cases which constitute the center of variation of the concept of referring and then examine the borderline cases in light of their similarities and differences from the paradigms. As long as we are aware of *both* similarities and differences, it may not matter much whether we call such cases referring or not.

To sum up: the speech act of referring is to be explained by giving examples of paradigmatic referring expressions, by explaining the function which the utterance of these expressions serves in the complete speech act (the illocutionary act), and by contrasting the use of these expressions with other expressions. Paradigmatic referring expressions in English fall into three classes as far as the surface structure of English sentences is concerned: proper names, noun phrases beginning with the definite article or a possessive pronoun or noun and followed by a singular noun, and pronouns. The utterance of a referring expression characteristically serves to pick out or identify a particular object apart from other objects. The use of these expressions is to be contrasted not only with the use of predicate expressions and complete sentences, but also with indefinite referring expressions, expressions referring to universals, and plural definite referring expressions. It should not be supposed that the boundaries of the concept of definite reference are precise.

2.4 *Propositions*

Whenever two illocutionary acts contain the same reference and predication, provided that the meaning of the referring expression is the same, I shall say the same proposition is expressed.[1] Thus, in the utterances of all of 1–5, the same proposition is expressed. And similarly in the utterances of:

6. If Sam smokes habitually, he will not live long.
7. The proposition that Sam smokes habitually is un-interesting.

the same proposition is expressed as in 1–5, though in both 6 and 7 the proposition occurs as part of another proposition. Thus *a proposition is to be sharply distinguished from an assertion or statement of it*, since in utterances of 1–7 the same proposition occurs, but only in 1 and 5 is it asserted. Stating and asserting are acts, but propositions are not acts. A proposition is what is asserted in the act of asserting, what is stated in the act of stating. The same point in a different way: an assertion is a (very special kind of) commitment to the truth of a proposition.

The expression of a proposition is a propositional act, not an illocutionary act. And as we saw, propositional acts cannot occur alone. One cannot just express a proposition while doing nothing else and have thereby performed a complete speech act. One grammatical correlate of this point is that clauses beginning with "that...", which are a characteristic form for explicitly isolating propositions, are not complete sentences. When a proposition is expressed it is always expressed in the performance of an illocutionary act.[2]

Notice that I do not say that the sentence expresses a proposition; I do not know how sentences could perform acts of that (or any other) kind. But I shall say that in the utterance of the sentence, the speaker expresses a proposition.

---

[1] This states a sufficient but could not state a necessary condition. Existential statements, e.g., have no reference.

[2] Thus, corresponding to the distinction between the act of stating and the statement made, is the distinction between the act of expressing a proposition and the proposition expressed.

I might summarize this part of my set of distinctions by saying that I am distinguishing between the illocutionary act and the propositional content of the illocutionary act. Of course not all illocutionary acts have a propositional content, for example, an utterance of "Hurrah" does not, nor does "Ouch".

The reader familiar with the literature will recognize this as a variation of an old distinction which has been marked by authors as diverse as Frege, Sheffer, Lewis, Reichenbach and Hare, to mention only a few.

From this semantical point of view we can distinguish two (not necessarily separate) elements in the syntactical structure of the sentence, which we might call the propositional indicator and the illocutionary force indicator. The illocutionary force indicator shows how the proposition is to be taken, or to put it another way, what illocutionary force the utterance is to have; that is, what illocutionary act the speaker is performing in the utterance of the sentence. Illocutionary force indicating devices in English include at least: word order, stress, intonation contour, punctuation, the mood of the verb, and the so-called performative[1] verbs. I may indicate the kind of illocutionary act I am performing by beginning the sentence with "I apologize", "I warn", "I state", etc. Often, in actual speech situations, the context will make it clear what the illocutionary force of the utterance is, without its being necessary to invoke the appropriate explicit illocutionary force indicator.

If this semantic distinction is of any real importance, it seems likely that it should have some syntactic analogue, even though the syntactical representation of the semantic facts will not always lie on the surface of the sentence. For example, in the sentence, "I promise to come", the surface structure does not seem to allow us to make a distinction between the indicator of illocutionary force and the indicator of propositional content. In this respect, it differs from, "I promise that I will come", where the difference between the indicator of illocutionary force ("I promise") and the indicator of propositional content ("that I will come") lies right on the surface. But if we study the deep structure of the first sentence, we find that its underlying phrase marker, like the underlying phrase marker of the second, contains, "I promise + I will come". In the deep structure we can often identify those elements that

---

[1] Austin, *op. cit.* pp. 4 ff. for an explanation of this notion.

correspond to the indicator of illocutionary force quite separately from those that correspond to the indicator of propositional content, even in cases where, e.g., deletion transformations of repeated elements conceal the distinction in the surface structure. This is not to say, of course, that there is in general some single element in the underlying phrase marker of every sentence which marks its illocutionary force. On the contrary, it seems to me that in natural languages illocutionary force is indicated by a variety of devices, some of them fairly complicated syntactically.

This distinction between illocutionary force indicators and proposition indicators will prove very useful to us in chapter 3, when we construct an analysis of an illocutionary act. Since the same proposition can be common to different kinds of illocutionary acts, we can separate our analysis of the proposition from our analysis of kinds of illocutionary acts. There are rules for expressing propositions, rules for such things as reference and predication, but I think that those rules can be discussed independently of the rules for illocutionary force indicating, and I shall postpone their discussion until chapters 4 and 5.

We can represent these distinctions in the following symbolism. The general form of (very many kinds of) illocutionary acts is

$$F(p)$$

where the variable "F" takes illocutionary force indicating devices as values and "p" takes expressions for propositions.[1] We can then symbolize different kinds of illocutionary acts in the forms, e.g.,

$\vdash(p)$	for assertions	$!(p)$	for requests
$Pr(p)$	for promises	$W(p)$	for warnings
	$?(p)$	for yes-no questions	

And so on. Except for yes-no questions the symbolism for questions must represent propositional functions and not complete propositions, because except in yes-no questions a speaker asking a question does not express a complete proposition. Thus, "How many people were at the party?" is represented as

$$?(X \text{ number of people were at the party})$$

"Why did he do it?" is represented as

$$?(\text{He did it because}\dots)$$

---

[1] Not all illocutionary acts would fit this model. E.g. "Hurrah for Manchester United" or "Down with Caesar" would be of the form $F(n)$, where "n" is replaceable by referring expressions.

For Searle every kind of sentence, 1-7, contains a prop., but each have different illocutionary forces! Thus, each are sentences.

But "Did you do it?", a yes-no question, is represented as

$$?(You\ did\ it)$$

In so far as we confine our discussion to simple subject predicate propositions, with a singular definite referring term as subject, we can represent the distinctions in the form

$$F\ (RP)$$

"R" for the referring expression and the capital "P" for the predicating expression.

An additional and powerful motivation for making these distinctions is that they enable us to account for and represent the generally overlooked distinction between illocutionary negation and propositional negation, the distinction between

$$\sim F(p)$$

and

$$F\ (\sim p)$$

Thus, e.g., the sentence, "I promise to come" has two negations, "I do not promise to come" and "I promise not to come". The former is an illocutionary negation, the latter a propositional negation. Propositional negations leave the character of the illocutionary act unchanged because they result in another proposition presented with the same illocutionary force. Illocutionary negations in general change the character of the illocutionary act. Thus, an utterance of "I do not promise to come" is not a promise but a refusal to make a promise. An utterance of "I am not asking you to do it" is a denial that a request is being made and is quite different from the negative request "Don't do it". The same distinction applies to statements. Consider the statement "There are horses".

$$\vdash (\exists x)(x\ is\ a\ horse)$$

In addition to the usual distinctions between, "There aren't any horses"

$$\vdash \sim (\exists x)(x\ is\ a\ horse)$$

and, "There are things that aren't horses",

$$\vdash (\exists x) \sim (x\ is\ a\ horse)$$

we need to add, "I don't say there are horses".

$$\sim \vdash (\exists x)(x\ is\ a\ horse)$$

32

It is tempting, but a mistake, to think that the negation of an illocutionary force indicating device leaves us with a negative assertion about the speaker, concerning his non-performance of some illocutionary act. That

is always really of the form
$$\sim F(p)$$
$$\vdash (\sim q)$$

On this account the refusal to perform an illocutionary act would always be a statement of an autobiographical kind to the effect that one did not as a matter of empirical fact perform such and such an act. But, e.g., "I don't promise" in "I don't promise to come" is no more an autobiographical claim than "I promise" is in "I promise to come".

Having divided up (a large number of types of) illocutionary acts into the elements represented by the letters in the notation "*F(RP)*", we can then offer separate analyses of illocutionary force (*F*), referring (*R*) and predicating (*P*). I shall discuss these three topics in chapters 3, 4 and 5 respectively. It is important to emphasize the limitations on the scope of the enterprise. We shall be dealing with very simple illocutionary acts of the sort that involve reference to a single object (usually in the utterance of a singular noun phrase) and the predication of simple expressions. I am ignoring more complex types of subject expressions, relational predicate expressions, and molecular propositions. Until we can get clear about the simple cases we are hardly likely to get clear about the more complicated ones.

2.5 *Rules*

I want to clarify a distinction between two different sorts of rules, which I shall call *regulative* and *constitutive* rules. I am fairly confident about the distinction, but do not find it easy to clarify. As a start, we might say that regulative rules regulate antecedently or independently existing forms of behavior; for example, many rules of etiquette regulate inter-personal relationships which exist independently of the rules. But constitutive rules do not merely regulate, they create or define new forms of behavior. The rules of football or chess, for example, do not merely regulate playing football or chess, but as it were they create the very possibility of playing such games. The activities of playing football or chess are constituted by acting in accordance with (at least a large subset of) the appropriate rules.[1] Regulative rules regulate a pre-existing activity, an activity whose existence is logically independent of the rules. Constitutive rules constitute (and also regulate) an activity the existence of which is logically dependent on the rules.

Regulative rules characteristically take the form of or can be paraphrased as imperatives, e.g., "When cutting food, hold the knife in the right hand", or "Officers must wear ties at dinner". Some constitutive rules take quite a different form, e.g., "A checkmate is made when the king is attacked in such a way that no move will leave it unattacked", "A touch-down is scored when a player has possession of the ball in the opponents' end zone while a play is in progress". If our paradigms of rules are imperative regulative rules, such non-imperative constitutive rules are likely to strike us as extremely curious and hardly even as rules at all. Notice that they are almost tautological in character, for what the 'rule' seems to offer is part of a definition of "checkmate" or "touchdown". That, for example, a checkmate in chess is achieved in such and such a way can appear now as a rule, now as an analytic truth based on the meaning of "checkmate in chess". That such statements can be construed as analytic is a clue to the fact that the rule in question is a constitutive one. The rules for checkmate or touchdown must 'define' *checkmate in chess* or *touchdown in American football* in the same way that the rules of football define "football" or the rules of chess define "chess"—which does not, of course, mean that a slight change in a fringe rule makes it a different game; there will be degrees of centrality in any system of constitutive rules. Regulative rules characteristically have the form or can be comfortably paraphrased in the form "Do X" or "If Y do X". Within systems of constitutive rules, some will have this form, but some

---

[1] This statement has to be understood in a certain way. When I say that playing, e.g. chess, consists in acting in accordance with the rules, I intend to include far more than just those rules that state the possible moves of the pieces. One could be following those rules and still not be playing chess, if for example the moves were made as part of a religious ceremony, or if the moves of chess were incorporated into some larger, more complex, game. In the notion of "acting in accordance with the rules", I intend to include the rules that make clear the 'aim of the game'. Furthermore, I think there are some rules crucial to competitive games which are not peculiar to this or that game. For example I think it is a matter of rule of competitive games that each side is committed to trying to win. Notice in this connection that our attitude to the team or player who deliberately throws the game is the same as that toward the team or player who cheats. Both violate rules, though the rules are of quite different sorts.

will have the form "*X* counts as *Y*", or "*X* counts as *Y* in context *C*".

The failure to perceive the existence and nature of constitutive rules is of some importance in philosophy. Thus, for example, some philosophers ask, "How can making a promise create an obligation?" A similar question would be, "How can scoring a touchdown create six points?" As they stand both questions can only be answered by citing a rule of the form, "*X* counts as *Y*", which is, of course, not to say that the questions cannot be re-phrased to ask important questions about the institution of promising—or for that matter, football.

The distinction as I have tried to sketch it is still rather vague, and I shall try to clarify it by commenting on the two formulae I have used to characterize constitutive rules: "The creation of constitutive rules, as it were, creates the possibility of new forms of behavior", and "constitutive rules often have the form: *X* counts as *Y* in context *C*".

"*New forms of behavior*": There is a trivial sense in which the creation of any rule creates the possibility of new forms of behavior, namely, behavior done as in accordance with the rule. That is not the sense in which my remark is intended. What I mean can perhaps be best put in the formal mode. Where the rule is purely regulative, behavior which is in accordance with the rule could be given the same description or specification (the same answer to the question "What did he do?") whether or not the rule existed, provided the description or specification makes no explicit reference to the rule. But where the rule (or system of rules) is constitutive, behavior which is in accordance with the rule can receive specifications or descriptions which it could not receive if the rule or rules did not exist. I shall illustrate this with examples.

Suppose that in my social circle it is a rule of etiquette that invitations to parties must be sent out at least two weeks in advance. The specification of the action, "He sent out the invita-tions at least two weeks in advance", can be given whether or not that rule exists. Suppose, also, that in my athletic circle football is a game played according to such and such rules. Now, the speci-fication, "They played football", cannot be given if there were no such rules. It is possible that twenty-two men might go through the same physical movements as are gone through by two teams at a football game, but if there were no rules of football, that is, no antecedently existing game of football, there is no sense in which their behavior could be described as playing football.

In general, social behavior could be given the same specifications even if there were no rules of etiquette. But constitutive rules, such as those for games, provide the basis for specifications of behavior which could not be given in the absence of the rule. Of course, regulative rules often provide the basis for appraisals of behavior, e.g., "He was rude", "He was immoral", "He was polite", and perhaps these appraisals could not be given unless backed up by some such rules. But appraisals are not *specifications* or *descriptions* as I am now using those phrases. "He voted for Willkie", and "He hit a home run", are specifications which could not be given without constitutive rules, but "He wore a tie at dinner", "He held his fork in his right hand", and "He sat down", are all specifications which could be given whether or not any rules requiring ties at dinner or right-handed fork use, etc., existed at all.[1]

"*X counts as Y in context C*": This is not intended as a formal criterion for distinguishing constitutive and regulative rules. Any regulative rule could be twisted into this form, e.g., "Non-wearing of ties at dinner counts as wrong officer behavior". But here the noun phrase following "counts as" is used as a term of appraisal not of specification. Where the rule naturally can be phrased in this form and where the *Y* term is a specification, the rule is likely to be constitutive. But there are two qualifications that need to be made. First, since constitutive rules come in systems, it may be the whole system which exemplifies this form and not individual rules within the system. Thus, though rule 1 of basketball—the game is played with five players to a side—does not lend itself to this form, acting in accordance with all or a sufficiently large subset of the rules does count as playing basketball. And secondly, within systems the phrase which is the *Y* term will not in general simply be a label. It will mark something that has consequences. Thus "offside", "homerun", "touchdown", "checkmate" are not mere labels for the state of affairs that is specified by the *X* term, but they introduce further consequences, by way of, e.g., penalties, points, and winning and losing.

I have said that the hypothesis of this book is that speaking a

---

[1] It is possible that artifacts in general require constitutive rules to be describable as, e.g., "tie" or "fork" in the first place. I do not believe they do, but I do not consider this problem here as it is irrelevant to my present concerns.

language is performing acts according to rules. The form this hypothesis will take is that the semantic structure of a language may be regarded as a conventional realization of a series of sets of underlying constitutive rules, and that speech acts are acts characteristically performed by uttering expressions in accordance with these sets of constitutive rules. One of the aims of the next chapter is to formulate sets of constitutive rules for the performances of certain kinds of speech acts, and if what I have said concerning constitutive rules is correct we should not be surprised if not all these rules take the form of imperative rules. Indeed, we shall see that the rules fall into several quite different categories, none of which is quite like the rules of etiquette. The effort to state the rules for the performance of speech acts can also be regarded as a test of the hypothesis that there are constitutive rules underlying speech acts. If we are unable to give any satisfactory rule formulations, our failure could be construed as partially disconfirming evidence against the hypothesis.

The sense in which I want to say that constitutive rules are involved in speaking a language can be made clearer if we consider the following question: What is the difference between making promises and, say, fishing that makes me want to say that doing the first in a language is only made possible by the existence of constitutive rules concerning the elements of a language and doing the second requires no analogous set of constitutive rules? After all, both promising and fishing are human activities (practices), both are goal-directed behavior, both allow for mistakes. A crucial part of the difference is this: In the case of fishing the ends-means relations, i.e. the relations that facilitate or enable me to reach my goal, are matters of natural physical facts; such facts, for example, as that fish sometimes bite at worms but very seldom at empty hooks; hooks made of steel hold fish, hooks made of butter do not. Now there are, indeed, techniques, procedures and even strategies that successful fishermen follow, and no doubt in some sense all these involve (regulative) rules. But that under such and such conditions one catches a fish is not a matter of convention or anything like a convention. In the case of speech acts performed within a language, on the other hand, it is a matter of convention —as opposed to strategy, technique, procedure, or natural fact— that the utterance of such and such expressions under certain conditions counts as the making of a promise.

37

"But", it might be objected, "you have still only told us how things like promising differ from things like fishing, and that is not sufficient to give any clear sense to your remarks about rules." I think this objection has real force and I want now to try to explain further what I mean when I say that the hypothesis of this book is that speaking a language is a matter of performing speech acts according to systems of constitutive rules. Let us begin by distinguishing three questions to which that remark is relevant. As an initial approximation we might pose them as follows: First, are languages (as opposed to language) conventional? Second, are illocutionary acts rule governed? Third, is language rule governed? I hope the proposed answers will make the questions clearer. The answer to the first is obviously yes. I am writing this according to the conventions of English and not, say, those of French, German, or Swahili. In that sense languages (as opposed to language) are conventional. But the second question is harder and more important. Let us rephrase it slightly. Must there be some conventions or other (French, German, or what have you) in order that one can perform illocutionary acts, such as stating, promising, requesting? And I want to say that the answer to that is, in general, yes.

Some very simple sorts of illocutionary acts can indeed be performed apart from any use of any conventional devices at all, simply by getting the audience to recognize certain of one's intentions in behaving in a certain way.[1] And these possibilities show us the limitations and weaknesses of the analogy with games, for one cannot, e.g., score a touchdown at all apart from invoking certain conventions (rules). But the fact that one can perform some illocutionary acts while standing outside a natural language, or any other system of constitutive rules, should not obscure the fact that in general illocutionary acts are performed within language in virtue of certain rules, and indeed could not be performed unless language allowed the possibility of their performance. One can in certain special circumstances 'request' someone to leave the room without employing any conventions, but unless one has a language one cannot request of someone that he, e.g., undertake a research project on the problem of diagnosing and treating mononucleosis in undergraduates in American universities. Furthermore, I wish to argue, some system of rule governed elements is necessary for there to be certain *types*

---

[1] Such cases are more limited than one might suppose. Facial expressions and gestures such as pointing have a heavy element of convention.

of speech act, such as promising or asserting. My dog can perform certain simple illocutionary acts. He can express pleasure and he can ask (request) that he be let out. But his range is very limited, and even for the types he can perform, one feels it is partly metaphorical to describe them as illocutionary acts at all.

To complete my answer to the second question, and to begin to answer the third, I wish to introduce two imaginary cases for the purpose of illustrating certain relations between rules, acts, and conventions.

First, imagine that chess is played in different countries according to different conventions. Imagine, e.g., that in one country the king is represented by a big piece, in another the king is smaller than the rook. In one country the game is played on a board as we do it, in another the board is represented entirely by a sequence of numbers, one of which is assigned to any piece that 'moves' to that number. Of these different countries, we could say that they play the same game of chess according to different conventional forms. Notice, also, that the rules must be realized in some form in order that the game be playable. Something, even if it is not a material object, must represent what we call the king or the board.

Secondly, imagine a society of sadists who like to cause each other pain by making loud noises in each others' ears. Suppose that for convenience they adopt the convention of always making the noise BANG to achieve this purpose. Of this case, like the chess case, we can say that it is a practice involving a convention. But unlike the chess case, the convention is not a realization of any underlying constitutive rules. Unlike the chess case, the conventional device is a device to achieve a natural effect. There is no rule to the effect that saying BANG *counts as* causing pain; one can feel the pain whether or not one knows the conventions. And pain still can be caused without employing any conventions.

Now, how about languages, language and illocutionary acts? Like both the chess case and the noise case, languages involve conventions. (My answer to the first question.) But I want to say, in regard to my second and third questions, that speaking a language and performing illocutionary acts are like the chess case in ways that they are crucially unlike the noise case. Different human languages, to the extent they are inter-translatable, can be regarded as different conventional realizations of the same underlying rules. The fact that in French one can make a promise by saying "je promets" and in English one can make it by saying "I promise" is a matter of convention. But the fact that an utterance of a promising device (under appropriate conditions) counts as the undertaking of an obligation is a matter of rules and not a matter of the conventions of French or English. Just as in the above example, we can translate a chess game in one country into a chess game of another because they share the same underlying rules, so we can translate utterances of one language into another because they share the same underlying rules. (It ought, incidentally, to be regarded as an extraordinary fact, one requiring an explanation, that sentences in one language can be translated into sentences in another language.)

Furthermore, to turn back to the second question, for many kinds of illocutionary acts there must be some conventional device or other for performing the act, because the act can be performed only within the rules and there must be some way of invoking the underlying rules. For the case of promises and statements there must be some conventional elements the utterance of which counts as an undertaking of an obligation or the commitment to the existence of some state of affairs in order for it to be possible to perform such speech acts as promising or stating. The things specified in the rules are not natural effects, like feeling a pain, which one can cause apart from invoking any rules at all. It is in this sense that I want to say that not only are languages conventional, but certain kinds of illocutionary acts are rule governed.

So, what my three questions amount to is: First, are there conventions for languages? Second, must there be rules (realized somehow) in order that it be possible to perform this or that illocutionary act? And third, are the conventions realizations of rules?

My answer to the first is yes, and my answer to the second is that for most kinds of illocutionary acts, yes they are rule governed, and for most acts, even within the other kinds, yes. My answer to the third question is, in general, yes.

The point of the analogies is that the noise case illustrates what it is for a practice to have a conventional mode of performance, without having constitutive rules and without requiring rules or conventions to perform the act. The chess case illustrates what it is for a practice to have conventional modes of performance, where the conventions are realizations of underlying rules, and where the rules and some conventions or other are required to perform the acts at all.

When I say that speaking a language is engaging in a rule-governed form of behavior, I am not especially concerned with the particular conventions one invokes in speaking this language or that (and it is primarily for this reason that my investigation differs fundamentally from linguistics, construed as an examination of the actual structure of natural human languages) but the underlying rules which the conventions manifest or realize, in the sense of the chess example. Now, when I say that speaking a language is engaging in a rule-governed form of behavior it is in the sense of an answer to question three that I intend this remark. Even if it should turn out that I am wrong about question two, that illocutionary acts all can be performed standing outside any system of constitutive rules, it still would not follow that performing them in a language is not engaging in a rule-governed form of behavior. I hold both views, but it is only the answer to question three which is crucial to my enterprise in this essay, because it is that view which articulates the hypothesis that *speaking a language* is engaging in a rule-governed form of behavior.

Two final questions about rules: *First*, must there be a penalty for its violation if the rule is a genuine one? Must all rules be thus normative? No. Not all constitutive rules have penalties; after all, what penalty is there for violating the rule that baseball is played with nine men on a side? Indeed, it is not easy to see how one could even violate the rule as to what constitutes checkmate in chess, or touchdown in football. *Secondly*, can one follow a rule without knowing it? It bothers some people that I claim that there are rules of language which we *discover* even though, I claim, we have been following them all along. But take an obvious phonological example: In my dialect, "linger" does not rhyme with "singer", nor "anger" with "hanger", though from the spelling it looks as though these pairs ought to rhyme. But "linger" and "anger" have a /g/ phoneme following the /ŋ/ phoneme, "singer" and "hanger" have only the /ŋ/ phoneme, thus /sɪŋər/ but /lɪŋgər/. If you get a list of examples like this, you will see that there is a rule: Wherever the word is formed from a verb the /g/ phoneme does not occur; where it is not so formed the /g/ is separately pronounced. Thus "sing": "singer"; "hang": "hanger"; "bring": "bringer"; but "linger", "anger", "finger", "longer" do not come from any verbs "ling", "ang", "fing", and "long". Further-more, I want to claim that this is a rule and not just a regularity, as can be seen both from the fact that we recognize departures as 'mispronunciations' and from the fact that the rule covers new cases, from its projective character. Thus, suppose we invent a noun "longer" from the verb "to long". "Longer" = df. *one who longs*. Then in the sentence, "This longer longs longer than that longer", the initial and terminal "longer" have no /g/ phoneme in their pronunciation, the interior "longer" however has the hard /g/. Not all English dialects have this rule, and I do not claim there are no exceptions—nonetheless, it is a good rule. It seems obvious to me that it is a rule, and that it is one which we follow without necessarily knowing (in the sense of being able to formu-late) that we do.

The implications of such examples for the present investigation are these. Sometimes in order to explain adequately a piece of human behavior we have to suppose that it was done in accordance with a rule, even though the agent himself may not be able to state the rule and may not even be conscious of the fact that he is acting in accordance with the rule. The agent's knowing how to do something may only be adequately explicable on the hypothesis that he knows (has acquired, internalized, learned) a rule to the effect that such and such, even though in an important sense he may not know that he knows the rule or that he does what he does in part because of the rule. Two of the marks of rule-governed as opposed to merely regular behavior are that we generally recognize deviations from the pattern as somehow wrong or defective and that the rule unlike the past regularity automatically covers new cases. Confronted with a case he has never seen before, the agent knows what to do.

2.6 *Meaning*

Illocutionary acts are characteristically performed in the utterance of sounds or the making of marks. What is the difference between *just* uttering sounds or making marks and performing an illocu-tionary act? One difference is that the sounds or marks one makes in the performance of an illocutionary act are characteristically said to *have meaning*, and a second related difference is that one is characteristically said to *mean something* by the utterance of those sounds or marks. Characteristically, when one speaks one means something by what one says; and what one says, the string of sounds that one emits, is characteristically said to have a meaning. Here, incidentally, is another point at which our analogy between performing speech acts and playing games breaks down. The pieces in a game like chess are not characteristically said to have a meaning, and furthermore, when one makes a move one is not characteristically said to mean anything by that move.

But what is it for one to mean something by what one says, and what is it for something to have a meaning? To answer the first of these questions, I propose to borrow and revise some ideas of Paul Grice. In an article entitled *Meaning*,[1] Grice gives the following analysis of the notion of "non-natural meaning".[2] To say that a speaker *S* meant something by *X* is to say that *S* intended the utterance of *X* to produce some effect in a hearer *H* by means of the recognition of this intention. Though I do not think this an adequate account, for reasons to be made clear later, I think it is a very useful beginning of an account of meaning, first because it makes a connection between meaning and intention, and secondly because it captures the following essential feature of linguistic communication. In speaking I attempt to communicate certain things to my hearer by getting him to recognize my intention to communicate just those things. I achieve the intended effect on the hearer by getting him to recognize my intention to achieve that effect, and as soon as the hearer recognizes what it is my intention to achieve, it is in general achieved. He understands what I am saying as soon as he recognizes my intention in uttering what I utter as an intention to say that thing.

I shall illustrate this with a simple example. When I say "Hello", I intend to produce in a hearer the knowledge that he is being greeted. If he recognizes it as my intention to produce in him that knowledge, then he thereby acquires that knowledge.

However valuable this account of meaning is, it seems to me to be defective in at least two crucial respects. First, it fails to account for the extent to which meaning can be a matter of rules or conventions. This account of meaning does not show the connection between one's meaning something by what one says, and what that which one says actually means in the language. Secondly, by

[1] *Philosophical Review* (July 1957), pp. 377–88.

[2] He distinguishes "meaning *nn*" (i.e. "non-natural meaning") from such senses of "mean" as occur in "Clouds mean rain" and "Those spots mean measles".

defining meaning in terms of intended effects it confuses illocutionary with perlocutionary acts. Put crudely, Grice in effect defines meaning in terms of intending to perform a perlocutionary act, but saying something and meaning it is a matter of intending to perform an illocutionary, not necessarily a perlocutionary, act. I shall now explain both these objections and attempt to amend Grice's account to deal with them.

In order to illustrate the first point, I shall present a counter-example to this analysis of meaning. The point of the counter-example will be to illustrate the connection between what a speaker means and what the words he utters mean.

Suppose that I am an American soldier in the Second World War and that I am captured by Italian troops. And suppose also that I wish to get these troops to believe that I am a German soldier in order to get them to release me. What I would like to do is to tell them in German or Italian that I am a German soldier. But let us suppose I don't know enough German or Italian to do that. So I, as it were, attempt to put on a show of telling them that I am a German soldier by reciting those few bits of German I know, trusting that they don't know enough German to see through my plan. Let us suppose I know only one line of German which I remember from a poem I had to memorize in a high school German course. Therefore, I, a captured American, address my Italian captors with the following sentence: *Kennst du das Land wo die Zitronen blühen?*[1] Now, let us describe the situation in Gricean terms. I intend to produce a certain effect in them, namely, the effect of believing that I am a German soldier, and I intend to produce this effect by means of their recognition of my intention. I intend that they should think that what I am trying to tell them is that I am a German soldier. But does it follow from this account that when I say, *Kennst du das Land*...*etc.*, what I mean is, "I am a German soldier"? Not only does it not follow, but in this case I find myself disinclined to say that when I utter the German sentence what I mean is "I am a German soldier", or even "Ich

---

[1] If it seems implausible that one could intend to produce the desired effects with such an utterance in these circumstances, a few imaginative additions to the example should make the case more plausible, e.g., I know that my captors know there are German soldiers in the area wearing American uniforms. I know that they have been instructed to be on the lookout for these Germans and to release them as soon as they identify themselves. I know that they have lied to their commander by telling him that they can speak German when in fact they cannot, etc.

bin ein deutscher Soldat", because what the words mean and what I remember that they mean is "Knowest thou the land where the lemon trees bloom?" Of course, I want my captors to be deceived into thinking that what I mean is: "I am a German soldier", but part of what is involved in that is getting them to think that that is what the words I utter mean in German. In the *Philosophical Investigations*,[1] Wittgenstein (discussing a different problem) writes "*Say* "it's cold here" and *mean* "it's warm here"". The reason we are unable to do this without further stage setting is that what we can mean is at least sometimes a function of what we are saying. Meaning is more than a matter of intention, it is also at least sometimes a matter of convention. One might say that on Grice's account it would seem that any sentence can be uttered with any meaning whatever, given that the circumstances make possible the appropriate intentions. But that has the consequence that the meaning of the sentence then becomes just another circumstance.

Grice's account can be amended to deal with counter-examples of this kind. We have here a case where I intend to produce a certain effect by means of getting the hearer's recognition of my intention to produce that effect, but the device I use to produce this effect is one which is conventionally, by the rules governing the use of that device, used as a means of producing quite different illocutionary effects, and the stage setting or conditions which would permit us to say one thing and mean something totally unrelated are not present. We must, therefore, reformulate the Gricean account of meaning in such a way as to make it clear that one's meaning something when one utters a sentence is more than just randomly related to what the sentence means in the language one is speaking. In our analysis of illocutionary acts, we must capture both the intentional and the conventional aspects and especially the relationship between them. In the performance of an illocutionary act in the literal utterance of a sentence, the speaker intends to produce a certain effect by means of getting the hearer to recognize his intention to produce that effect; and furthermore, if he is using words literally, he intends this recognition to be achieved in virtue of the fact that the rules for using the expressions he utters associate the expression with the production of that effect. It is this *combination* of elements which we shall need to express in our analysis of the illocutionary act.

[1] Para. 510.

45

I now turn to my second objection to Grice's account. In effect, the account says that saying something and meaning it is a matter of intending to perform a perlocutionary act. In the examples Grice gives, the effects cited are invariably perlocutionary. I wish to argue that saying something and meaning it is a matter of intending to perform an illocutionary act. First, it could not be the case that in general intended effects of meant utterances were perlocutionary because many kinds of sentences used to perform illocutionary acts have no perlocutionary effect associated with their meaning. For example, there is no associated perlocutionary effect of greeting. When I say "Hello" and mean it, I do not necessarily intend to produce or elicit any state or action in my hearer other than the knowledge that he is being greeted. But that knowledge is simply his *understanding* what I said, it is not an additional response or effect. Furthermore, there is no perlocutionary effect of, for example, promising which will distinguish promises from firm statements of intention and emphatic predictions. All three tend to create expectations in the hearer about the future, but "I promise" does not mean "I predict" or "I intend". Any account of meaning must show that when I say "I promise" or "Hello" and mean it, I mean it in exactly the same sense of "mean" as when I say "Get out" and mean it. Yet Grice's account seems to suit only the last of these three sentences, since it is the only one whose meaning is such that in the ordinary cases the speaker who utters and means it intends to produce an 'effect' on the hearer of the kind Grice discusses. The meaning of the sentence "Get out" ties it to a particular intended perlocutionary effect, namely getting the hearer to leave. The meanings of "Hello" and "I promise" do not.

Secondly, even where there generally is a correlated perlocutionary effect, I may say something and mean it without in fact intending to produce that effect. Thus, for example, I may make a statement without caring whether my audience believes it or not but simply because I feel it my duty to make it.

Third, it is not in general the case that when one speaks to someone with the intent of, e.g., telling him some item of information, that one intends that his reason, or even one of his reasons, for believing what one tells him should be that one intends him to believe it. When I read, say, a book of philosophy there are all sorts of reasons for believing or disbelieving what the author says, but it is not one of my reasons for believing what the author says that I recognize that he intends me to believe it. Nor, unless he is an extraordinarily egocentric author, will it have been his intention that I should believe it because I recognize that he intends me to believe it. The Gricean reflexive intention does not work for perlocutionary effects.

Well, then, how does it work? Let us remind ourselves of a few of the facts we are seeking to explain. Human communication has some extraordinary properties, not shared by most other kinds of human behavior. One of the most extraordinary is this: If I am trying to tell someone something, then (assuming certain conditions are satisfied) as soon as he recognizes that I am trying to tell him something and exactly what it is I am trying to tell him, I have succeeded in telling it to him. Furthermore, unless he recognizes that I am trying to tell him something and what I am trying to tell him, I do not fully succeed in telling it to him. In the case of illocutionary acts we succeed in doing what we are trying to do by getting our audience to recognize what we are trying to do. But the 'effect' on the hearer is not a belief or response, it consists simply in the hearer understanding the utterance of the speaker. It is this effect that I have been calling the illocutionary effect. The way the reflexive intention works then, as a preliminary formulation, is: the speaker S intends to produce an illocutionary effect IE in the hearer H by means of getting H to recognize S's intention to produce IE.[1]

The characteristic intended effect of meaning is understanding, but understanding is not the sort of effect that is included in Grice's examples of effects. It is not a perlocutionary effect. Nor can we amend Grice's account so that meaning is analyzed in terms of understanding. That would be too circular, for one feels that meaning and understanding are too closely tied for the latter to be the basis for an analysis of the former. So what I shall do in my analysis of illocutionary acts is unpack what constitutes under-

[1] This formulation incidentally avoids counter-examples of the type that Strawson adduces. (P. F. Strawson, 'Intention and convention in speech acts', *Philosophical Review* (October 1964), pp. 439–60.) In Strawson's example S intends to get H to believe something by means of getting H to recognize S's intention that he believes it. But S is not performing an illocutionary act at all. As soon as it is specified that the intention is to secure an illocutionary effect, that type of counter-example is eliminated. Of course, the further problem remains of specifying what an illocutionary effect is without circularity or an infinite regress of intentions, but that we shall have to tackle later.

standing a literal utterance in terms of (some of) the rules concerning the elements of the uttered sentence and in terms of the hearer's recognition of the sentence as subject to those rules.

My first and second objection to Grice's account hang together, and if they are valid the following picture should begin to emerge: On the speaker's side, saying something and meaning it are closely connected with intending to produce certain effects on the hearer. On the hearer's side, understanding the speaker's utterance is closely connected with recognizing his intentions. In the case of literal utterances the bridge between the speaker's side and the hearer's side is provided by their common language. Here is how the bridge works:

1. Understanding a sentence is knowing its meaning.

2. The meaning of a sentence is determined by rules, and those rules specify both conditions of utterance of the sentence and also what the utterance counts as.

3. Uttering a sentence and meaning it is a matter of (*a*) intending (*i*-1) to get the hearer to know (recognize, be aware of) that certain states of affairs specified by certain of the rules obtain, (*b*) intending to get the hearer to know (recognize, be aware of) these things by means of getting him to recognize *i*-1 [1] and (*c*) intending to get him to recognize *i*-1 in virtue of his knowledge of the rules for the sentence uttered.

4. The sentence then provides a conventional means of achieving the intention to produce a certain illocutionary effect in the hearer. If a speaker utters the sentence and means it he will have intentions (*a*), (*b*), and (*c*). The hearer's understanding the utterance will simply consist in those intentions being achieved. And the intentions will in general be achieved if the hearer understands the sentence, i.e., knows its meaning, i.e., knows the rules governing its elements.

Let us illustrate these points with a very simple example used earlier—an utterance of the sentence "Hello". 1. Understanding the sentence "Hello" is knowing its meaning. 2. The meaning of

---

[1] Cannot (*b*) be dispensed with altogether? I think not. Not only must *S* intend to produce *IE* by virtue of *H*'s knowing the meaning of the sentence, but he must also intend that *H* recognize the utterance of the sentence as one produced with the intention of producing *IE*. And that involves intending that he so recognize the utterance. Until he recognizes intention 1, *H* does not understand *S*. As soon as he does recognize intention 1, he does understand *S*. It seems, therefore, that the intention to produce understanding involves the intention that *H* should recognize intention 1.

"Hello" is determined by semantic rules, which specify both its conditions of utterance and what the utterance counts as. The rules specify that under certain conditions an utterance of "Hello" counts as a greeting of the hearer by the speaker. 3. Uttering "Hello" and meaning it is a matter of (*a*) intending to get the hearer to recognize that he is being greeted, (*b*) intending to get him to recognize that he is being greeted by means of getting him to recognize one's intention to greet him, (*c*) intending to get him to recognize one's intention to greet him in virtue of his knowledge of the meaning of the sentence "Hello". 4. The sentence "Hello" then provides a conventional means of greeting people. If a speaker says "Hello" and means it he will have intentions (*a*), (*b*), and (*c*), and from the hearer's side, the hearer's understanding the utterance will simply consist in those intentions being achieved. The intentions will be achieved in general if the hearer understands the sentence "Hello", i.e., understands its meaning, i.e., understands that under certain conditions its utterance counts as a greeting. In the characterization of the example, I used the word "greeting", which is the name of an illocutionary act, and so the example would be circular if it were presented by itself as an analysis of meaning, since the notion of greeting already involves the notion of meaning. But that is only a feature of the example and not of the analysis, since ultimately the analysis is in terms of rules and the hearer's knowledge of the rules and therefore makes no explicit use in the analysans of any term that involves "means" as part of its own meaning.

We can summarize the difference between the original Gricean analysis of meaning *nn* and my revised analysis of the different concept of saying something and meaning it as follows:

1. Grice's original analysis

   Speaker S means *nn* something by $X =$

   (*a*) S intends (i-1) the utterance U of X to produce a certain perlocutionary effect PE in hearer H.

   (*b*) S intends U to produce PE by means of the recognition of i-1.

2. Revised analysis

   S utters sentence T and means it (i.e., means literally what he says) =

   S utters T and

   (*a*) S intends (i-1) the utterance U of T to produce in H the knowledge (recognition, awareness) that the states of affairs specified by (certain of) the rules of T obtain. (Call this effect the illocutionary effect, IE)

(*b*) S intends U to produce IE by means of the recognition of i-1.

(*c*) S intends that i-1 will be recognized in virtue of (by means of) H's knowledge of (certain of) the rules governing (the elements of) T.

2.7 *The distinction between brute and institutional facts*

There is a certain picture we have of what constitutes the world and consequently of what constitutes knowledge about the world. The picture is easy to recognize but hard to describe. It is a picture of the world as consisting of brute facts, and of knowledge as really knowledge of brute facts. Part of what I mean by that is that there are certain paradigms of knowledge and that these paradigms are taken to form the model for all knowledge. The paradigms vary enormously—they range from "This stone is next to that stone" to "Bodies attract with a force inversely proportional to the square of the distance between them and directly proportional to the product of their mass" to "I have a pain", but they share certain common features. One might say they share the feature that the concepts which make up the knowledge are essentially physical, or, in its dualistic version, either physical or mental. The model for systematic knowledge of this kind is the natural sciences, and the basis for all knowledge of this kind is generally supposed to be simple empirical observations recording sense experiences.

It is obvious that large tracts of apparently fact-stating language do not consist of concepts which are part of this picture.[1] Notoriously, statements in ethics and esthetics are not readily assimilable to this picture, and philosophers who have accepted the picture have tended to deal with them either by saying that they were not statements at all but mere expressions of emotions, or that such statements were simply autobiographical statements of a psychological kind, recording, as Hume says, sentiments. It cannot be said that the implausibility of these ways of dealing with the problems posed by ethics and esthetics has been any bar

[1] Cf. G. E. M. Anscombe, 'On Brute Facts', *Analysis*, vol. 18, no. 3 (1958).

to their popularity, but their popularity is at least evidence of the power of the picture.

Leaving aside the question of the status of statements in ethics and esthetics, which are controversial areas anyway, there are many kinds of facts, and facts which obviously are objective facts and not matters of opinion or sentiment or emotion at all, which are hard, if not impossible, to assimilate to this picture. Any newspaper records facts of the following sorts: Mr Smith married Miss Jones; the Dodgers beat the Giants three to two in eleven innings; Green was convicted of larceny; and Congress passed the Appropriations Bill. There is certainly no easy way that the classical picture can account for facts such as these. That is, there is no simple set of statements about physical or psychological properties of states of affairs to which the statements of facts such as these are reducible. A marriage ceremony, a baseball game, a trial, and a legislative action involve a variety of physical movements, states, and raw feels, but a specification of one of these events only in such terms is not so far a specification of it as a marriage ceremony, baseball game, a trial, or a legislative action. The physical events and raw feels only count as parts of such events given certain other conditions and against a background of certain kinds of institutions.

Such facts as are recorded in my above group of statements I propose to call *institutional facts*. They are indeed facts; but their existence, unlike the existence of brute facts, presupposes the existence of certain human institutions. It is only given the institution of marriage that certain forms of behavior constitute Mr Smith's marrying Miss Jones. Similarly, it is only given the institution of baseball that certain movements by certain men constitute the Dodgers' beating the Giants 3 to 2 in eleven innings. And, at an even simpler level, it is only given the institution of money that I now have a five dollar bill in my hand. Take away the institution and all I have is a piece of paper with various gray and green markings.[1]

These "institutions" are systems of constitutive rules. Every institutional fact is underlain by a (system of) rule(s) of the form

---

[1] Brute facts, such as, e.g., the fact that I weigh 160 pounds, of course require certain conventions of measuring weight and also require certain linguistic institutions in order to be stated in a language, but the fact stated is nonetheless a brute fact, as opposed to the fact that it was stated, which is an institutional fact.

"*X* counts as *Y* in context *C*". Our hypothesis that speaking a language is performing acts according to constitutive rules involves us in the hypothesis that the fact that a man performed a certain speech act, e.g., made a promise, is an institutional fact. We are not, therefore, attempting to give an analysis of such facts in terms of brute facts.

In this connection, let us examine the inadequacy of the brute fact conception of knowledge to account for institutional facts. Let us investigate my thesis that the concepts which form the classical picture are not rich enough to describe institutional facts. To illustrate this inadequacy, imagine what it would be like to describe institutional facts in purely brute terms. Let us imagine a group of highly trained observers describing an American football game in statements only of brute facts. What could they say by way of description? Well, within certain areas a good deal could be said, and using statistical techniques certain 'laws' could even be formulated. For example, we can imagine that after a time our observer would discover the law of periodical clustering: at statistically regular intervals organisms in like colored shirts cluster together in a roughly circular fashion (the huddle). Further- more, at equally regular intervals, circular clustering is followed by linear clustering (the teams line up for the play), and linear clustering is followed by the phenomenon of linear interpenetra- tion. Such laws would be statistical in character, and none the worse for that. But no matter how much data of this sort we imagine our observers to collect and no matter how many inductive generalizations we imagine them to make from the data, they still have not described American football. What is missing from their description? What is missing are all those concepts which are backed by constitutive rules, concepts such as touchdown, offside, game, points, first down, time out, etc., and consequently what is missing are all the true statements one can make about a football game using those concepts. The missing statements are precisely what describes the phenomenon on the field *as a game of football*. The other descriptions, the descriptions of the brute facts, can be explained in terms of the institutional facts. But the institutional facts can only be explained in terms of the constitutive rules which underlie them.

No one, I guess, would try to offer a description of football in terms of brute facts, and yet, curiously enough, people have tried to offer semantic analyses of languages armed with only a conceptual structure of brute facts and ignoring the semantic rules that underlie the brute regularities. Some of these have a kind of *prima facie* plausibility, because there are regularities to be discovered in linguistic behavior, just as in our imagined 'scientific' study of football regularities turned up. But such regularities as do turn up, either in terms of regular correlations of stimulus and response (if I make the noise, "Is there any salt here?" when there is salt present; the subject makes the noise, "Yes") or in terms of correlations between utterances and states of affairs (the sound "Please pass the salt" is in general only uttered when and where there is salt present), must seem totally unexplained to anyone who holds the brute fact conception of semantics. The obvious explanation for the brute regularities of language (certain human made noises tend to occur in certain states of affairs or in the presence of certain stimuli) is that the speakers of a language are engaging in a rule-governed form of intentional behavior. The rules account for the regularities in exactly the same way that the rules of football account for the regularities in a game of football, and without the rules there seems no accounting for the regularities.

Chapter 3

THE STRUCTURE OF
ILLOCUTIONARY ACTS

The ground has now been prepared for a full dress analysis of the illocutionary act. I shall take promising as my initial quarry, because as illocutionary acts go, it is fairly formal and well articulated; like a mountainous terrain, it exhibits its geographical features starkly. But we shall see that it has more than local interest, and many of the lessons to be learned from it are of general application.

In order to give an analysis of the illocutionary act of promising I shall ask what conditions are necessary and sufficient for the act of promising to have been successfully and non-defectively performed in the utterance of a given sentence. I shall attempt to answer this question by stating these conditions as a set of propositions such that the conjunction of the members of the set entails the proposition that a speaker made a successful and non-defective promise, and the proposition that the speaker made such a promise entails this conjunction. Thus each condition will be a necessary condition for the successful and non-defective performance of the act of promising, and taken collectively the set of conditions will be a sufficient condition for such a performance. There are various kinds of possible defects of illocutionary acts but not all of these defects are sufficient to vitiate the act in its entirety. In some cases, a condition may indeed be intrinsic to the notion of the act in question and not satisfied in a given case, and yet the act will have been performed nonetheless. In such cases I say the act was "defective". My notion of a defect in an illocutionary act is closely related to Austin's notion of an "infelicity".[1] Not all of the conditions are logically independent of each other. Sometimes it is worthwhile to state a condition separately even though it is, strictly speaking, entailed by another.

If we get such a set of conditions we can extract from them a set of rules for the use of the illocutionary force indicating device. The

[1] J. L. Austin, *How to Do Things with Words* (Oxford, 1962), especially lectures II, III, IV.

54

method here is analogous to discovering the rules of chess by asking oneself what are the necessary and sufficient conditions under which one can be said to have correctly moved a knight or castled or checkmated a player, etc. We are in the position of someone who has learned to play chess without ever having the rules formulated and who wants such a formulation. We learned how to play the game of illocutionary acts, but in general it was done without an explicit formulation of the rules, and the first step in getting such a formulation is to set out the conditions for the performance of a particular illocutionary act. Our inquiry will therefore serve a double philosophical purpose. By stating a set of conditions for the performance of a particular illocutionary act we shall have offered an explication of that notion and shall also have paved the way for the second step, the formulation of the rules.

So described, my enterprise must seem to have a somewhat archaic and period flavor. One of the most important insights of recent work in the philosophy of language is that most non-technical concepts in ordinary language lack absolutely strict rules. The concepts of *game*, or *chair*, or *promise* do not have absolutely knockdown necessary and sufficient conditions, such that unless they are satisfied something cannot be a game or a chair or a promise, and given that they are satisfied in a given case that case must be, cannot but be, a game or a chair or a promise. But this insight into the looseness of our concepts, and its attendant jargon of "family resemblance"[1] should not lead us into a rejection of the very enterprise of philosophical analysis; rather the conclusion to be drawn is that certain forms of analysis, especially analysis into necessary and sufficient conditions, are likely to involve (in varying degrees) idealization of the concept analyzed. In the present case, our analysis will be directed at the center of the concept of promising. I am ignoring marginal, fringe, and partially defective promises. This approach has the consequence that counter-examples can be produced of ordinary uses of the word "promise" which do not fit the analysis. Some of these counter-examples I shall discuss. Their existence does not 'refute' the analysis, rather they require an explanation of why and how they depart from the paradigm cases of promise making.

Furthermore, in the analysis I confine my discussion to full blown explicit promises and ignore promises made by elliptical

[1] Cf. Ludwig Wittgenstein, *Philosophical Investigations* (New York, 1953), paras. 66,67.

turns of phrase, hints, metaphors, etc. I also ignore promises made in the course of uttering sentences which contain elements irrelevant to the making of the promise. I am also dealing only with categorical promises and ignoring hypothetical promises, for if we get an account of categorical promises it can easily be extended to deal with hypothetical ones. In short, I am going to deal only with a simple and idealized case. This method, one of constructing idealized models, is analogous to the sort of theory construction that goes on in most sciences, e.g., the construction of economic models, or accounts of the solar system which treat planets as points. Without abstraction and idealization there is no systematization.

Another difficulty with the analysis arises from my desire to state the conditions without certain forms of circularity. I want to give a list of conditions for the performance of a certain illocutionary act, which do not themselves mention the performance of any illocutionary acts. I need to satisfy this condition in order to offer a model for explicating illocutionary acts in general; otherwise I should simply be showing the relation between different illocutionary acts. However, although there will be no reference to illocutionary acts, certain institutional concepts, such as e.g. "obligation", will appear in the analysans as well as in the analysandum; I am not attempting to reduce institutional facts to brute facts, and thus there is no reductionist motivation in the analysis. Rather, I want to analyze certain statements of institutional facts, statements of the form "X made a promise", into statements containing such notions as intentions, rules, and states of affairs specified by the rules. Sometimes those states of affairs will themselves involve institutional facts.[1]

In the presentation of the conditions I shall first consider the case of a sincere promise and then show how to modify the conditions to allow for insincere promises. As our inquiry is semantical rather than syntactical, I shall simply assume the existence of grammatically well-formed sentences.

[1] Alston in effect tries to analyze illocutionary acts using only brute notions (except the notion of a rule). As he points out, his analysis is unsuccessful. I suggest that it could not be successful without involving institutional notions. Cf. W. P. Alston, 'Linguistic Acts', *American Philosophical Quarterly*, vol. 1, no. 2 (1964).

3.1 How to promise: a complicated way

Given that a speaker *S* utters a sentence *T* in the presence of a hearer *H*, then, in the literal utterance of *T*, *S* sincerely and non-defectively promises that *p* to *H* if and only if the following conditions 1–9 obtain:

1. *Normal input and output conditions obtain.*

I use the terms "input" and "output" to cover the large and indefinite range of conditions under which any kind of serious and literal[1] linguistic communication is possible. "Output" covers the conditions for intelligible speaking and "input" covers the conditions of understanding. Together they include such things as that the speaker and hearer both know how to speak the language; both are conscious of what they are doing; they have no physical impediments to communication, such as deafness, aphasia, or laryngitis; and they are not acting in a play or telling jokes, etc. It should be noted that this condition excludes *both* impediments to communication such as deafness and also parasitic forms of communication such as telling jokes or acting in a play.

2. *S expresses the proposition that p in the utterance of T.*

This condition isolates the proposition from the rest of the speech act and enables us to concentrate on the peculiarities of promising as a kind of illocutionary act in the rest of the analysis.

3. *In expressing that p, S predicates a future act A of S.*

In the case of promising the scope of the illocutionary force indicating device includes certain features of the proposition. In a promise an act must be predicated of the speaker and it cannot be a past act. I cannot promise to have done something, and I cannot promise that someone else will do something (although I can promise to see that he will do it). The notion of an act, as I am construing it for the present purposes, includes refraining from acts, performing series of acts, and may also include states and conditions: I may promise not to do something, I may promise to do somethings repeatedly or sequentially, and I may promise to be or remain in a certain state or condition. I call conditions 2 and 3 the propositional content conditions. Strictly speaking, since expressions and not acts are predicated of objects, this condition should be formulated as follows: In expressing that *P*, *S* predicates

---

[1] I contrast "serious" utterances with play acting, teaching a language, reciting poems, practicing pronunciation, etc., and I contrast "literal" with metaphorical, sarcastic, etc.

an expression of S, the meaning of which expression is such that if the expression is true of the object it is true that the object will perform a future act A.[1] But that is rather longwinded, so I have resorted to the above metonymy.

4. *H would prefer S's doing A to his not doing A, and S believes H would prefer his doing A to his not doing A.*

One crucial distinction between promises on the one hand and threats on the other is that a promise is a pledge to do something for you, not to you; but a threat is a pledge to do something to you, not for you. A promise is defective if the thing promised is something the promisee does not want done; and it is further defective if the promisor does not believe the promisee wants it done, since a non-defective promise must be intended as a promise and not as a threat or warning. Furthermore, a promise, unlike an invitation, normally requires some sort of occasion or situation that calls for the promise. A crucial feature of such occasions or situations seems to be that the promisee wishes (needs, desires, etc.) that something be done, and the promisor is aware of this wish (need, desire, etc.). I think both halves of this double condition are necessary in order to avoid fairly obvious counter-examples.[2]

One can, however, think of apparent counter-examples to this condition as stated. Suppose I say to a lazy student, "If you don't hand in your paper on time I promise you I will give you a failing grade in the course". Is this utterance a promise? I am inclined to think not; we would more naturally describe it as a warning or possibly even a threat. But why, then, is it possible to use the locution "I promise" in such a case? I think we use it here because "I promise" and "I hereby promise" are among the strongest illocutionary force indicating devices for *commitment* provided by the English language. For that reason we often use these expressions in the performance of speech acts which are not strictly speaking promises, but in which we wish to emphasize the degree of our commitment. To illustrate this, consider another apparent counter-example to the analysis along different lines. Sometimes one hears people say "I promise" when making an emphatic assertion. Suppose, for example, I accuse you of having stolen the money. I say, "You stole that money, didn't you?". You reply,

[1] Cf. the discussion of predication in chapter 2.
[2] For an interesting discussion of this condition, see Jerome Schneewind, 'A note on promising', *Philosophical Studies*, vol. 17, no. 3 (April 1966), pp. 33–5.

"No, I didn't, I promise you I didn't". Did you make a promise in this case? I find it very unnatural to describe your utterance as a promise. This utterance would be more aptly described as an emphatic denial, and we can explain the occurrence of the illocutionary force indicating device "I promise" as derivative from genuine promises and serving here as an expression adding emphasis to your denial.

In general, the point stated in condition 4 is that if a purported promise is to be non-defective, the thing promised must be something the hearer wants done, or considers to be in his interest, or would prefer being done to not being done, etc.; and the speaker must be aware of or believe or know, etc., that this is the case. I think a more elegant and exact formulation of this condition would probably require the introduction of technical terminology of the welfare economics sort.

5. *It is not obvious to both S and H that S will do A in the normal course of events.*

This condition is an instance of a general condition on many different kinds of illocutionary acts to the effect that the act must have a point. For example, if I make a request to someone to do something which it is obvious that he is already doing or is about to do quite independently of the request, then my request is pointless and to that extent defective. In an actual speech situation, listeners, knowing the rules for performing illocutionary acts, will assume that this condition is satisfied. Suppose, for example, that in the course of a public speech I say to a member of my audience, "Look here, Smith, pay attention to what I am saying". In interpreting this utterance, the audience will have to assume that Smith has not been paying attention, or at any rate that it is not obvious that he has been paying attention, that the question of his not paying attention has arisen in some way, because a condition for making non-defective request is that it is not obvious that the hearer is doing or about to do the thing requested.

Similarly with promises. It is out of order for me to promise to do something that it is obvious to all concerned that I am going to do anyhow. If I do make such a promise, the only way my audience can interpret my utterance is to assume that I believe that it is not obvious that I am going to do the thing promised. A happily married man who promises his wife he will not desert her in the next week is likely to provide more anxiety than comfort.

Parenthetically, I think this condition is an instance of the sort of phenomenon stated in Zipf's law. I think there is operating in our language, as in most forms of human behavior, a principle of least effort, in this case, a principle of maximum illocutionary ends with minimum phonetic effort; and I think condition 5 is an instance of it.

I call conditions such as 4 and 5 *preparatory conditions*. Though they do not state the essential feature, they are *sine quibus non* of happy promising.

6. *S intends to do A.*

The distinction between sincere and insincere promises is that, in the case of sincere promises, the speaker intends to do the act promised; in the case of insincere promises, he does not intend to do the act. Also, in sincere promises, the speaker believes it is possible for him to do the act (or to refrain from doing it), but I think the proposition that he intends to do it entails that he thinks it is possible to do (or refrain from doing) it, so I am not stating that as an extra condition. I call this condition the *sincerity condition*.

7. *S intends that the utterance of T will place him under an obligation to do A.*

The essential feature of a promise is that it is the undertaking of an obligation to perform a certain act. I think that this condition distinguishes promises (and other members of the same family such as vows) from other kinds of illocutionary acts. Notice that in the statement of the condition, we only specify the speaker's intention; further conditions will make clear how that intention is realized. It is clear, however, that having this intention is a necessary condition of making a promise, for if a speaker can demonstrate that he did not have this intention in a given utterance he can prove that the utterance was not a promise. We know, for example, that Mr Pickwick did not really promise to marry the woman because we know he did not have the appropriate intention. I call this the *essential condition*.

8. *S intends (i-1) to produce in H the knowledge (K) that the utterance of T is to count as placing S under an obligation to do A. S intends to produce K by means of the recognition of i-1, and he intends i-1 to be recognized in virtue of (by means of) H's knowledge of the meaning of T.*

This captures our amended Gricean analysis of what it is for the speaker to mean the utterance as a promise. The speaker intends to produce a certain illocutionary effect by means of getting the hearer to recognize his intention to produce that effect, and he also intends this recognition to be achieved in virtue of the fact that the meaning of the item he utters conventionally associates it with producing that effect. In this case the speaker assumes that the semantic rules (which determine the meaning) of the expressions uttered are such that the utterance counts as the undertaking of an obligation. The rules, in short, as we shall see in the next condition, enable the intention in the essential condition 7 to be achieved by making the utterance. And the articulation of that achievement, the way the speaker gets the job done, is described in condition 8.

9. *The semantical rules of the dialect spoken by S and H are such that T is correctly and sincerely uttered if and only if conditions 1–8 obtain.*[1]

This condition is intended to make clear that the sentence uttered is one which, by the semantical rules of the language, is used to make a promise. Taken together with condition 8, it eliminates counter-examples like the captured soldier example considered earlier. The meaning of a sentence is entirely determined by the meaning of its elements, both lexical and syntactical. And that is just another way of saying that the rules governing its utterance are determined by the rules governing its elements. We shall soon attempt to formulate the rules which govern the element or elements which serve to indicate that the illocutionary force is that of a promise.

I am construing condition 1 broadly enough so that together with the other conditions it guarantees that H understands the utterance, that is, together with 2–9 it entails that the illocutionary effect K is produced in H by means of H's recognition of S's intention to produce it, which recognition is achieved in virtue of H's knowledge of the meaning of T. This condition could always be stated as a separate condition, and if the reader thinks that I am asking too much of my input and output conditions that they should guarantee that the hearer understands the utterance, then he should treat this as a separate condition.

---

[1] As far as condition 1 is concerned, this is a bit misleading. Condition 1 is a general condition on any serious linguistic communication and is not peculiar to this or that dialect. Furthermore the use of the biconditional in this condition excludes ambiguous sentences. We have to assume that T is unambiguous.

3.2 *Insincere promises*

So far we have considered only the case of a sincere promise. But insincere promises are promises nonetheless, and we now need to show how to modify the conditions to allow for them. In making an insincere promise the speaker does not have all the intentions he has when making a sincere promise; in particular he lacks the intention to perform the act promised. However, he purports to have that intention. Indeed, it is because he purports to have intentions which he does not have that we describe his act as insincere.

A promise involves an expression of intention, whether sincere or insincere. So to allow for insincere promises, we need only to revise our conditions to state that the speaker takes responsibility for having the intention rather than stating that he actually has it. A clue that the speaker does take such responsibility is the fact that he could not say without absurdity, e.g., "I promise to do A but I do not intend to do A". To say, "I promise to do A" is to take responsibility for intending to do A, and this condition holds whether the utterance was sincere or insincere. To allow for the possibility of an insincere promise, then we have only to revise condition 6 so that it states not that the speaker intends to do A, but that he takes responsibility for intending to do A, and to avoid the charge of circularity, I shall phrase this as follows:

6a. *S intends that the utterance of T will make him responsible for intending to do A.*

Thus amended (and with "sincerely" dropped from our analysandum and from condition 9), our analysis is neutral on the question whether the promise was sincere or insincere.

3.3 *Rules for the use of the illocutionary force indicating device*

Our next task is to extract from our set of conditions a set of rules for the use of the indicator of illocutionary force. Obviously, not all of our conditions are equally relevant to this task. Condition 1 and conditions of the forms 8 and 9 apply generally to all kinds of normal illocutionary acts and are not peculiar to promising. Rules for the illocutionary force indicator for promising are to be found corresponding to conditions 2–7.

The semantical rules for the use of any illocutionary force indicating device Pr for promising are:

Rules for use of illocutionary force indicating device

Rule 1. Pr is to be uttered only in the context of a sentence (or larger stretch of discourse) T, the utterance of which predicates some future act A of the speaker S. I call this the *propositional content rule*. It is derived from the propositional content conditions 2 and 3.

Rule 2. Pr is to be uttered only if the hearer H would prefer S's doing A to his not doing A, and S believes H would prefer S's doing A to his not doing A.

Rule 3. Pr is to be uttered only if it is not obvious to both S and H that S will do A in the normal course of events. I call rules 2 and 3 *preparatory rules*, and they are derived from the preparatory conditions 4 and 5.

Rule 4. Pr is to be uttered only if S intends to do A. I call this the *sincerity rule*, and it is derived from the sincerity condition 6.

Rule 5. The utterance of Pr counts as the undertaking of an obligation to do A. I call this the *essential rule*.

These rules are ordered: rules 2–5 apply only if rule 1 is satisfied, and rule 5 applies only if rules 2 and 3 are satisfied as well. We shall see later on that some of these rules seem to be just particular manifestations as regards promising of very general underlying rules for illocutionary acts; and ultimately we should be able, as it were, to factor them out, so that they are not finally to be construed as rules exclusively for the illocutionary force indicating device for promising as opposed to other types of illocutionary force indicating devices.

Notice that whereas rules 1–4 take the form of quasi-imperatives, i.e., they are of the form: utter Pr only if x; rule 5 is of the form: the utterance of Pr counts as Y. Thus, rule 5 is of the kind peculiar to systems of constitutive rules which I discussed in chapter 2.

Notice also that the rather tiresome analogy with games is holding up remarkably well. If we ask ourselves under what conditions a player could be said to move a knight correctly, we would find preparatory conditions such as that it must be his turn to move, as well as the essential condition stating the actual positions the knight can move to. There are even sincerity conditions for competitive games, such as that one does not cheat or attempt to 'throw' the game. Of course, the corresponding sincerity 'rules' are not rules peculiar to this or that game but apply to competitive games generally. There usually are no propositional content rules for games, because games do not in general represent states of affairs.

To which elements, in an actual linguistic description of a natural language would rules such as 1–5 attach? Let us assume for the sake of argument that the general outlines of the Chomsky–Fodor–Katz–Postal[1] account of syntax and semantics are correct. Then it seems to me extremely unlikely that illocutionary act rules would attach directly to elements (formatives, morphemes) generated by the syntactic component, except in a few cases such as the imperative. In the case of promising, the rules would more likely attach to some output of the combinatorial operations of the semantic component. Part of the answer to this question would depend on whether we can reduce all illocutionary acts to some very small number of basic illocutionary types. If so, it would then seem somewhat more likely that the deep structure of a sentence would have a simple representation of its illocutionary type.

3.4 *Extending the analysis*

If this analysis is of any general interest beyond the case of promising, then it would seem that these distinctions should carry over into other types of illocutionary act, and I think a little reflection will show that they do. Consider, e.g., giving an order. The preparatory conditions include that the speaker should be in a position of authority over the hearer, the sincerity condition is that the speaker wants the ordered act done, and the essential condition has to do with the fact that the speaker intends the utterance as an attempt to get the hearer to do the act. For assertions, the preparatory conditions include the fact that the hearer must have some basis for supposing the asserted proposition is true, the sincerity condition is that he must believe it to be true, and the essential condition has to do with the fact that the proposition is presented as representing an actual state of affairs. Greetings are a much simpler kind of speech act, but even here some of the distinctions apply. In the utterance of "Hello" there is no propositional content and no sincerity condition. The preparatory condition is that the speaker must have just encountered the hearer, and the essential rule is that the utterance counts as a

[1] Cf., e.g., J. Katz and P. Postal, *An Integrated Theory of Linguistic Descriptions* (Cambridge, Mass., 1964).

courteous indication of recognition of the hearer. We can represent such information about a wide range of illocutionary acts in the table shown on pp. 66–7.

On the basis of this table, it is possible to formulate and test certain general hypotheses concerning illocutionary acts:

1. Wherever there is a psychological state specified in the sincerity condition, the performance of the act counts as an *expression* of that psychological state. This law holds whether the act is sincere or insincere, that is whether the speaker actually has the specified psychological state or not. Thus to assert, affirm, state (that *p*) counts as an *expression of belief* (that *p*). To request, ask, order, entreat, enjoin, pray, or command (that *A* be done) counts as *an expression of a wish or desire* (that *A* be done). To promise, vow, threaten or pledge (that *A*) counts as *an expression of intention* (to do *A*). To thank, welcome or congratulate counts as *an expression of gratitude*, *pleasure* (at *H*'s arrival), or *pleasure* (at *H*'s good fortune).[1]

2. The converse of the first law is that only where the act counts as the expression of a psychological state is insincerity possible. One cannot, for example, greet or christen insincerely, but one can state or promise insincerely.

3. Where the sincerity condition tells us what the speaker *expresses* in the performance of the act, the preparatory condition tells us (at least part of) what he *implies* in the performance of the act. To put it generally, in the performance of any illocutionary act, the speaker implies that the preparatory conditions of the act are satisfied. Thus, for example, when I make a statement I imply that I can back it up, when I make a promise, I imply that the thing promised is in the hearer's interest. When I thank someone, I imply that the thing I am thanking him for has benefited me (or was at least intended to benefit me), etc.

It would be nicely symmetrical if we could give an account of *saying* in terms of the essential rules, parallel to our accounts of *implying* and *expressing*. The temptation is to say: the speaker *implies* the (satisfaction of the) preparatory conditions, *expresses* the (state specified in the) sincerity conditions, and *says* (whatever is specified by) the essential condition. The reason this breaks down

---

[1] This law, incidentally, provides the solution to Moore's paradox: the paradox that I cannot assert both that *p* and that I do not believe *p*, even though the proposition that *p* is not inconsistent with the proposition that I do not believe *p*.

Types of illocutionary act

	Request	Assert, state (that), affirm	Question[1]
Types of rule Propositional content	Future act A of H.	Any proposition p.	Any proposition or propositional function.
Preparatory	1. H is able to do A. S believes H is able to do A. 2. It is not obvious to both S and H that H will do A in the normal course of events of his own accord.	1. S has evidence (reasons, etc.) for the truth of p. 2. It is not obvious to both S and H that H knows (does not need to be reminded of, etc.) p.	1. S does not know 'the answer', i.e., does not know if the proposition is true, or, in the case of the propositional function, does not know the information needed to complete the proposition truly (but see comment below). 2. It is not obvious to both S and H that H will provide the information at that time without being asked.
Sincerity	S wants H to do A.	S believes p.	S wants this information.
Essential	Counts as an attempt to get H to do A.	Counts as an undertaking to the effect that p represents an actual state of affairs.	Counts as an attempt to elicit this information from H.
Comment:	Order and command have the additional preparatory rule that S must be in a position of authority over H. Command probably does not have the 'pragmatic' condition requiring non-obviousness. Furthermore in both, the authority relationship infects the essential condition because the utterance counts as an attempt to get H to do A in virtue of the authority of S over H.	Unlike argue these do not seem to be essentially tied to attempting to convince. Thus "I am simply stating that p and not attempting to convince you" is acceptable, but "I am arguing that p and not attempting to convince you" sounds inconsistent.	There are two kinds of questions, (a) real questions, (b) exam questions. In real questions S wants to know (find out) the answer; in exam questions, S wants to know if H knows.

	Thank (for)	Advise	Warn
Propositional content	Past act *A* done by *H*.	Future act *A* of *H*.	Future event or state, etc., *E*.
Preparatory	*A* benefits *S* and *S* believes *A* benefits *S*.	1. *S* has some reason to believe *A* will benefit *H*. 2. It is not obvious to both *S* and *H* that *H* will do *A* in the normal course of events.	1. *H* has reason to believe *E* will occur and is not in *H*'s interest. 2. It is not obvious to both *S* and *H* that *E* will occur.
Sincerity	*S* feels grateful or appreciative for *A*.	*S* believes *A* will benefit *H*.	*S* believes *E* is not in *H*'s best interest.
Essential	Counts as an expression of gratitude or appreciation.	Counts as an undertaking to the effect that *A* is in *H*'s best interest.	Counts as an undertaking to the effect that *E* is not in *H*'s best interest.
Comment:	Sincerity and essential rules overlap. Thanking is just expressing gratitude in a way that, e.g., promising is not just expressing an intention.	Contrary to what one might suppose advice is not a species of requesting. It is interesting to compare "advise" with "urge", "advocate" and "recommend". Advising you is not trying to get you to do something in the sense that requesting is. Advising is more like telling you what is best for you.	Warning is like advising, rather than requesting. It is not, I think, necessarily an attempt to get you to take evasive action. Notice that the above account is of categorical not hypothetical warnings. Most warnings are probably hypothetical: "If you do not do X then Y will occur."

	Greet	Congratulate
Propositional content	None.	Some event, act, etc., *E* related to *H*.
Preparatory	*S* has just encountered (or been introduced to, etc.) *H*.	*E* is in *H*'s interest and *S* believes *E* is in *H*'s interest.
Sincerity	None.	*S* is pleased at *E*.
Essential	Counts as courteous recognition of *H* by *S*.	Counts as an expression of pleasure at *E*.
Comment:		"Congratulate" is similar to "thank" in that it is an expression of its sincerity condition.

1 In the sense of "ask a question" not in the sense of "doubt".

is that there is a close connection between saying and the constative class of illocutionary acts. Saying fits statements but not greetings. Indeed, Austin's original insight into performatives was that some utterances were not sayings, but doings of some other kind. But this point can be exaggerated. A man who says "I (hereby) promise" not only promises, but *says* he does.[1] That is, there is indeed a connection between saying and constatives, but it is not as close as one might be inclined to think.

4. It is possible to perform the act without invoking an explicit illocutionary force-indicating device where the context and the utterance make it clear that the essential condition is satisfied. I may say only "I'll do it for you", but that utterance will count as and will be taken as a promise in any context where it is obvious that in saying it I am accepting (or undertaking, etc.) an obligation. Seldom, in fact, does one actually need to say the explicit "I promise". Similarly, I may say only "I wish you wouldn't do that", but this utterance in certain contexts will be more than merely an expression of a wish, for, say, autobiographical purposes. It will be a request. And it will be a request in those contexts where the point of saying it is to get you to stop doing something, i.e., where the essential condition for a request is satisfied.

This feature of speech—that an utterance in a context can indicate the satisfaction of an essential condition without the use of the explicit illocutionary force-indicating device for that essential condition—is the origin of many polite turns of phrase. Thus, for example, the sentence, "Could you do this for me?" in spite of the meaning of the lexical items and the interrogative illocutionary force-indicating devices is not characteristically uttered as a subjunctive question concerning your abilities; it is characteristically uttered as a request.

5. Wherever the illocutionary force of an utterance is not explicit it can always be made explicit. This is an instance of the principle of expressibility, stating that whatever can be meant can be said. Of course, a given language may not be rich enough to enable speakers to say everything they mean, but there are no barriers in principle to enriching it. Another application of this law is that whatever can be implied can be said, though if my

[1] As J. L. Austin himself points out, 'Other minds', *Proceedings of the Aristotelian Society*, supplementary vol. (1964); reprinted in J. L. Austin, *Philosophical Papers* (Oxford, 1961).

account of preparatory conditions is correct, it cannot be said without implying other things.

6. The overlap of conditions on the table shows us that certain kinds of illocutionary acts are really special cases of other kinds; thus asking questions is really a special case of requesting, viz., requesting information (real question) or requesting that the hearer display knowledge (exam question). This explains our intuition that an utterance of the request form, "Tell me the name of the first President of the United States", is equivalent in force to an utterance of the question form, "What's the name of the first President of the United States?" It also partly explains why the verb "ask" covers both requests and questions, e.g., "He asked me to do it" (request), and "He asked me why" (question).

A crucially important but difficult question is this: Are there some basic illocutionary acts to which all or most of the others are reducible? Or alternatively: What are the basic species of illocutionary acts, and within each species what is the principle of unity of the species? Part of the difficulty in answering such questions is that the principles of distinction which lead us to say in the first place that such and such is a different kind of illocutionary act from such and such other act are quite various (see 8 below).[1]

7. In general the essential condition determines the others. For example, since the essential rule for requesting is that the utterance counts as an attempt to get H to do something, then the propositional content rule has to involve future behavior of H.

If it really is the case that the other rules are functions of the essential rule, and if some of the others tend to recur in consistent patterns, then these recurring ones ought to be eliminable. In particular the non-obviousness preparatory condition runs through so many kinds of illocutionary acts that I think that it is not a matter of separate rules for the utterance of particular illocutionary force-indicating devices at all, but rather is a general condition on illocutionary acts (and analogously for other kinds of behavior) to the effect that the act is defective if the point to be achieved by the satisfaction of the essential rule is already achieved. There is, e.g., no point in telling somebody to do something if it is completely obvious that he is going to do it anyhow. But that is no more a *special* rule for requests than it is a matter of a special rule

---

[1] In this respect, Austin's classification of illocutionary acts into five categories seems somewhat *ad hoc. How to Do Things with Words*, pp. 150 ff.

for moving the knight that the player can only move the knight when it is his turn to move.

8. The notions of illocutionary force and different illocutionary acts involve really several quite different principles of distinction. First and most important, there is the point or purpose of the act (the difference, for example, between a statement and a question); second, the relative positions of S and H (the difference between a request and an order); third, the degree of commitment undertaken (the difference between a mere expression of intention and a promise); fourth, the difference in propositional content (the difference between predictions and reports); fifth, the difference in the way the proposition relates to the interest of S and H (the difference between boasts and laments, between warnings and predictions); sixth, the different possible expressed psychological states (the difference between a promise, which is an expression of intention, and a statement, which is an expression of belief); seventh, the different ways in which an utterance relates to the rest of the conversation (the difference between simply replying to what someone has said and objecting to what he has said). So we must not suppose, what the metaphor of "force" suggests, that the different illocutionary verbs mark off points on a single continuum. Rather, there are several different continua of 'illocutionary force', and the fact that the illocutionary verbs of English stop at certain points on these various continua and not at others is, in a sense, accidental. For example, we might have had an illocutionary verb "rubrify", meaning to call something "red". Thus, "I hereby rubrify it" would just mean "It's red". Analogously, we happen to have an obsolete verb "macarize", meaning to call someone happy.[1]

Both because there are several different dimensions of illocutionary force, and because the same utterance act may be performed with a variety of different intentions, it is important to realize that one and the same utterance may constitute the performance of several different illocutionary acts. There may be several different non-synonymous illocutionary verbs that correctly characterize the utterance. For example suppose at a party a wife says "It's really quite late". That utterance may be at one level a statement of fact; to her interlocutor, who has just remarked on how early it was,

[1] I owe the former of these examples to Paul Grice, the latter to Peter Geach, 'Ascriptivism', *Philosophical Review*, vol. 69 (1960), pp. 221–6.

it may be (and be intended as) an objection; to her husband it may be (and be intended as) a suggestion or even a request (" Lets go home ") as well as a warning (" You'll feel rotten in the morning if we don't ").

9. Some illocutionary verbs are definable in terms of the intended perlocutionary effect, some not. Thus requesting is, as a matter of its essential condition, an attempt to get a hearer to do something, but promising is not essentially tied to such effects on or responses from the hearer. If we could get an analysis of all (or even most) illocutionary acts in terms of perlocutionary effects, the prospects of analyzing illocutionary acts without reference to rules would be greatly increased. The reason for this is that language could then be regarded as just a conventional means for securing or attempting to secure natural responses or effects. The illocutionary act would then not essentially involve any rules at all. One could in theory perform the act in or out of a language, and to do it in a language would be to do with a conventional device what could be done without any conventional devices. Illocutionary acts would then be (optionally) conventional but not rule governed at all.

As is obvious from everything I have said, I think this reduction of the illocutionary to the perlocutionary and the consequent elimination of rules probably cannot be carried out. It is at this point that what might be called institutional theories of communication, like Austin's, mine, and I think Wittgenstein's, part company with what might be called naturalistic theories of meaning, such as, e.g., those which rely on a stimulus-response account of meaning.

Chapter 4

REFERENCE AS A SPEECH ACT

In this chapter and the next we shall delve inside the proposition to consider the propositional acts of reference and predication. Our discussion of reference will be confined to singular definite reference and will be to that extent an incomplete theory of reference. As we shall see that alone will provide us with plenty of problems, but until we get clear about them we are hardly likely to get clear about other kinds of reference.

The notion of singular definite reference is a very unsatisfactory one, but one we can hardly do without. The most obvious cases of referring expressions are proper names, but as soon as we consider other kinds of expressions such as singular definite descriptions we find that some of them are referring expressions, some obviously not, and some seem to fall in between. Furthermore, some occurrences of proper names are not referential, as in, e.g., "Cerberus does not exist". Philosophers who discuss definite descriptions almost invariably fasten onto examples like "the king of France", or "the man", and seldom onto examples like "the weather", "the way we live now", or "the reason why I like beans". This ought to arouse our suspicions. Consider for example the difficulty of applying Russell's theory of descriptions, without any paraphrases of the original, to a sentence like "The weather is good": "$(\exists x)$ (x is a weather· (y) (y is a weather $\rightarrow y = x$)· x is good)" hardly makes any sense. Yet one is inclined to say the expression "the weather" performs a similar role in "The weather is good" to that of the expression "the man" in "The man is good".

Let us consider some occurrences of definite descriptions which are clearly not referential occurrences. In an utterance of "He left me in the lurch" the expression "the lurch" is not used to refer. Similarly in "I did it for his sake" the expression "his sake" is not used to refer.[1] We can see this more obviously by contrasting the occurrence of "the lurch" and "his sake" in these sentences with the occurrences of "the building" and "his brother" in the

---

[1] This example is from W. Quine, *Word and Object* (Cambridge, 1960), p. 236.

sentences "He left me in the building" and "I did it for his brother". Still, how do I know that the former pair do not and the latter pair do refer? I know that because, as a native speaker, I can see that the utterances of the former pair do not serve to pick out or identify some object or entity and that utterances of the latter pair do. This fact has certain interesting linguistic consequences, and to someone who could not see the obvious lack of reference of "the lurch" and "the sake", pointing out these consequences might be an aid. For example, the first pair are not answers to the corresponding question forms: "For whom or what of his did I do it?" and "In what did he leave me?", whereas the latter pair clearly do answer such questions. Furthermore, in these sorts of contexts, "sake" and "lurch" do not admit of plural forms, whereas "brother" and "building" do. From the point of view of a generative syntax we might say that "his sake" and "the lurch" are not noun phrases at all and "sake" and "lurch" are not nouns in these occurrences.

Another source of complexity is that not all referential occurrences of singular referring expressions are, so to speak, categorical. Some are hypothetical. Thus, in an utterance of "He will inherit the money", "he" is used to refer categorically. But in an utterance of "If they have a son, he will inherit the money", "he" refers only contingently on the truth of the antecedent proposition. Similar cases can be constructed using proper names, e.g., "If the queen of England has a son named Henry, then Henry will be the youngest of five children". In what follows I shall be investigating categorical reference, just as in the case of promising I investigated categorical rather than hypothetical promises.

4.1 *Use and Mention*

Not every occurrence of a referring expression in discourse is a referring occurrence as we noted in the last section. Furthermore, sometimes expressions, whether referring expressions or otherwise, occur in discourse without having their normal use but are themselves talked about in the discourse. Thus consider the difference between:

1. Socrates was a philosopher; and
2. "Socrates" has eight letters.

Comparing these sentences two facts are obvious: first, the same word begins both sentences, and second, the role that the word plays in an utterance of the sentence is quite different in the two cases, since in 1 it has its normal use to refer to a particular man and in 2 it does not have its normal use, but rather is talked about—as is indicated by the presence of the quotation marks. In their efforts to account for the difference in such cases philosophers and logicians have sometimes, in fact usually, been led to deny the obvious truth that the same word begins both sentences.

A very confused account of the distinction between the use and the mention of expressions is so commonly held that it is worth trying briefly to clarify the matter. It is generally claimed by philosophers and logicians that in a case like 2 the word "Socrates" does not occur at all, rather a completely new word occurs, the proper name of the word. Proper names of words or other expressions, they claim, are formed by putting quotation marks around the expression, or rather, around what would be the expression if it were a use of the expression and not just a part of a new proper name. On this account, the word which begins 2 is not, as you might think, "Socrates", it is ""Socrates"". And the word I just wrote, elusively enough, is not ""Socrates"", but is """Socrates""" which completely new word is yet another proper name of a proper name of a proper name, namely """"Socrates"""". And so on up in a hierarchy of names of names of names....

I find this account absurd. And I believe it is not harmlessly so but rests on a profound miscomprehension of how proper names, quotation marks, and other elements of language really work. Furthermore, it has infected other areas of the philosophy of language. For example, clauses beginning with the word "that" are sometimes erroneously said to be proper names of propositions, on analogy with the orthodox account of use and mention.

There are at least two ways to show that the orthodox account of use and mention must be false. The first is to point out certain general features of the institution of proper names which count against it. The second is to contrast what it would actually be like to refer to expressions with proper names or definite descriptions with the way we use quotation marks to present the expression itself.

If we ask ourselves why we have the institution of proper names at all, part of the answer is that we need a convenient device for making identifying references to commonly referred to objects when the objects are not always themselves present. But the device has no point when the object we wish to talk about is itself a stretch of discourse, and hence is easily produceable and does not require a separate linguistic device to refer to it. With very few exceptions, such as sacred words or obscenities, if we wish to speak of a word we don't need to name it or otherwise refer to it, we can simply produce (a token of) it. The odd cases where we do need names of words are those cases where it is improper or taboo or inconvenient to produce the word itself. We have conventions in written discourse, e.g., quotation marks, to mark the fact that the word is not being used normally but is being used as a topic of discussion. In short, we have the institution of proper names to talk in words about things which are not themselves words and which need not be present when they are being talked about. The whole institution gets its point from the fact that we use words to refer to other objects. A proper name can only be a proper name if there is a genuine difference between the name and the thing named. If they are the same, the notion of naming and referring can have no application.

Contrast what it is like to actually refer to a word with the way we talk about a word in 2. Suppose we rewrite 2 to read

> The word which is the name of Plato's most famous teacher has eight letters.

Here, as distinct from 2, we genuinely use a definite description to *refer* to a word. Or we can imagine giving a proper name to a word; let, e.g., "John" be the name of the word "Socrates", then we can again rewrite 2 as

> John has eight letters.

Here "John" is used as a genuine proper name and is used to refer to an object other than itself, namely "Socrates".

But when we want to talk about a word it is almost always possible to produce the word itself, as in 2. It would be redundant to have a name for it as well, and it would be false to construe it as the name or as part of the name of itself. But how then shall we characterize the utterance of the first word in 2? The answer is quite simple: a word is here uttered but not in its normal use. The word itself is *presented* and then talked about, and that it is to be taken as presented and talked about rather than used conventionally to refer is indicated by the quotes. But the word is not referred to, nor does it refer to itself.

"Well," it might be said, "why can't we just adopt it as a convention that quotation marks around a word make a new word out of it, the proper name of the original?" One might as well say, why not adopt it as a convention that in the sentence "Snow is white", "is" is the name of my grandmother. The fact is, we already have conventions governing the use of quotation marks. One (only one) of them is that words surrounded by quotation marks are to be taken as talked about (or quoted, etc.) and not as used by the speaker in their normal use. Anyone wishing to introduce a new convention owes us first an account of how it squares with such existing conventions, and secondly, what motivates the introduction of the new convention. But first, since we already have perfectly adequate use-mention conventions, it is not clear how the proposed new convention is going to relate to them without inconsistency. Secondly, if one searches in the literature for any motivation for the 'convention' that quotation marks around a word or other expression make a completely new proper name one finds only various false views about language, e.g., "the fundamental conventions regarding the use of any language require that in any utterance we make about an object it is the name of the object which must be employed, and not the object itself. In consequence if we wish to say something about a sentence, for example, that it is true, we must use the name of this sentence, and not the sentence itself."[1] One's only reply can be that there is no such fundamental convention. Bits of discourse or other oral or visually presentable items can quite easily occur in discourse as the topic of the discourse. For example, an ornithologist might say, "The sound made by the California Jay is..." And what completes the sentence is a sound, not a proper name of a sound.

---

[1] A. Tarski, 'The semantic conception of truth', *Philosophy and Phenomenological Research*, vol. 4 (1944); reprinted in H. Feigl and W. Sellars (eds.), *Readings in Philosophical Analysis* (New York, 1949).

4.2 *Axioms of reference*

Keeping in mind the fact that not every occurrence of a referring expression is a referring occurrence, we now want to give an analysis of definite reference parallel to our analysis of illocutionary acts in the last chapter. Unlike most speech acts, reference has a long history of treatment by philosophers, going back at least as far as Frege (and really as far back as Plato's *Theaetetus*, if not earlier), so we shall want to work up to our analysis fairly carefully, surveying a good deal of the philosophical scenery along the way. The theory we shall present is in the tradition that begins with Frege and continues in Strawson's *Individuals*, and, as the reader will see, is heavily influenced by those two authors.

There are two generally recognized axioms concerning referring and referring expressions. As a rough formulation we might state them as follows:

    1. Whatever is referred to must exist.[1]

Let us call this the axiom of existence.

    2. If a predicate is true of an object it is true of anything identical with that object regardless of what expressions are used to refer to that object.

Let us call this the axiom of identity.

Both of these can be interpreted in ways which render them tautologies. The first is an obvious tautology since it says only that one cannot refer to a thing if there is no such thing to be referred to. The second too admits of a tautological interpretation, as saying that whatever is true of an object is true of that object.

Both of these axioms give rise to paradoxes, the first because of confusions about what it is to refer, the second because some of its re-interpretations are not tautologies but falsehoods. The first produces paradoxes about such statements as, e.g., "The Golden Mountain does not exist". If we conjointly assume the axiom of existence and that the first three words of this sentence are used to refer, then the statement becomes self-defeating for, in order to state it, it must be false. In order for me to deny the existence of anything it must exist.

---

[1] "Exist" has to be construed tenselessly. One can refer to what has existed or what will exist as well as to what now exists.

Russell[1] dissolved this paradox by pointing out (in effect) that the expression "the Golden Mountain" is not used to refer when it is the grammatical subject of an existential proposition. In general, subject expressions in existential sentences cannot be used to refer—this is part of what is meant by saying that existence is not a property—and therefore no paradox arises. The axiom of existence does not apply because there is no reference. Unfortunately in his enthusiasm Russell denied in effect that any definite description could be used to refer. I shall criticize this part of his argument later.[2] Thanks to Russell no one takes these paradoxes seriously any more.

But it might still seem that counter-examples could be produced to this axiom. Can't one refer to Santa Claus and Sherlock Holmes, though neither of them exists or ever did exist? References to fictional (and also legendary, mythological, etc.) entities are not counter-examples. One can refer to them *as fictional characters* precisely because they do *exist in fiction*. To make this clear we need to distinguish normal real world talk from parasitic forms of discourse such as fiction, play acting, etc. In normal real world talk I cannot refer to Sherlock Holmes because there never was such a person. If in this 'universe of discourse' I say "Sherlock Holmes wore a deerstalker hat" I fail to refer, just as I would fail to refer if I said "Sherlock Holmes is coming to dinner tonight at my house". Neither statement can be true. But now suppose I shift into the fictional, play acting, let's-pretend mode of discourse. Here if I say "Sherlock Holmes wore a deerstalker hat", I do indeed refer to a fictional character (i.e. a character who does not exist but who exists in fiction) and what I say here is true. Notice that in this mode of discourse I cannot say "Sherlock Holmes is coming to my house for dinner tonight", for the reference to "my house" puts me back in real world talk. Furthermore, if in the fictional mode of discourse I say, "Mrs Sherlock Holmes wore a deerstalker hat" I fail to refer for there is no fictional Mrs Sherlock Holmes. Holmes, to speak in the fictional mode, never got married. In short, in real world talk both "Sherlock Holmes" and "Mrs Sherlock Holmes" fail of reference because there never existed any such people. In fictional talk "Sherlock Holmes" refers, for such a character really does exist in fiction, but "Mrs Sherlock Holmes" fails of

[1] B. Russell, 'On denoting', *Mind*, vol. 14 (1905); reprinted in Feigl and Sellars (eds.), *op. cit.*   [2] In chapter 7.

reference for there is no such fictional character. The axiom of existence holds across the board: in real world talk one can refer only to what exists; in fictional talk one can refer to what exists in fiction (plus such real world things and events as the fictional story incorporates).

So stated these points must seem fairly obvious, but the philosophical literature really does reveal an extraordinary amount of confusion on these matters. To forestall two more confusions, I should emphasize that my account of parasitic forms of discourse does not involve the view that there are any changes in the *meanings* of words or other linguistic elements in fictional discourse. If we think of the meaning conventions of linguistic elements as being (at least in part) vertical conventions, tying sentences to the world, then it is best to think of the tacit conventions of fictional discourse as being lateral or horizontal conventions lifting, as it were, the discourse away from the world. But it is essential to realize that even in "Little Red Riding Hood", "red" means red. The conventions of fiction don't change the meaning of words or other linguistic elements. Secondly, the fact that there is such a fictional character as Sherlock Holmes does not commit us to the view that he exists in some suprasensible world or that he has a special mode of existence. Sherlock Holmes does not exist at all, which is not to deny that he exists-in-fiction.

The axiom of identity (as well as the axiom of existence) gives rise to further paradoxes and puzzles in referentially opaque contexts. This axiom is sometimes[1] stated as follows: If two expressions refer to the same object they can be substituted for each other in all contexts *salva veritate*. In this form this is not a tautology but a falsehood and it is in this form that it is so troublesome. I think that these puzzles are as trivial as those arising out of the axiom of existence, but to expose them is quite a lengthy affair and goes beyond the scope of this book.

The next aim of this chapter is not to continue discussion of these two axioms, but to add a third and to explore some of its consequences.

3. If a speaker refers to an object, then he identifies or is able on demand to identify that object for the hearer apart from all other objects.

[1] E.g. R. Carnap, *Meaning and Necessity*, pp. 98 ff.

Let us call this the axiom of identification. This axiom too is a tautology, since it only serves to articulate my exposition of the notion of (singular, definite) reference. It admits of the following formulation.

3*a*. A necessary condition for the successful performance of a definite reference in the utterance of an expression is that either the utterance of that expression must communicate[1] to the hearer a description true of, or a fact about, one and only one object, or if the utterance does not communicate such a fact the speaker must be able to substitute an expression, the utterance of which does.

There are only three ways in which a speaker can guarantee that such a fact be communicated: Either the expression uttered must contain predicates true of only one object, or its utterance together with the context must provide some ostensive or indexical presentation of one and only one object, or its utterance must provide a mixture of indexical indicators and descriptive terms sufficient to identify one and only one object. If the expression uttered is not one of these, the reference can only be successful on the condition that the speaker is able to produce one of these on demand. To have another name, let us call this the principle of identification.

This is not so obviously tautological. Indeed, at first sight it may not even seem plausible and will certainly need explication before it is even clear. Nonetheless, it seems to me an important truth, and indeed one with a history, for it is nothing more than a generalization of Frege's dictum that every referring expression must have a sense.

I am now going to argue toward establishing this principle by examining the necessary conditions for the performance of the speech act of definite reference. In so doing I shall try to show a logical connection between the axiom of existence and the axiom of identification.

---

[1] "Communicate" is not always the most appropriate verb. To say that the speaker communicates a fact to the hearer suggests that the hearer was previously unaware of the fact communicated. But often in referring, the proposition "communicated" to the hearer is one he already knows to be true. Perhaps we should say the speaker "appeals to", or "invokes" a proposition in such cases. I shall however continue to use "communicate" or "convey" with the proviso that they are not to be taken as suggesting the hearer's prior ignorance of what is communicated or conveyed.

4.3   *Kinds of definite referring expressions*

Let us begin by isolating the kinds of expressions under consideration. *Grammatically* they divide roughly into four categories.

1. Proper names, e.g., "Socrates", "Russia".
2. Complex noun phrases in the singular.

The latter often contain a relative clause and often, though not always, begin with a definite article, e.g., "the man who called", "the highest mountain in the world", "France's present crisis". Borrowing and slightly expanding Russell's term, I shall continue to call these "*definite descriptions*". The expressions following the "the" I shall call "*descriptors*", and in cases where no definite article appears the whole expression will be called a descriptor. In no sense is this terminology intended to imply a philosophical analysis or theory about the notions of "describing" and "descriptions": they are arbitrary terms used for convenience. Note that a definite description may contain another definite referring expression, either another definite description, or an expression of another type such as a proper name, e.g., "John's brother". "the woman who is married to the man who is drunk". In such expressions I shall call the referent of the whole expression the *primary* referent, and the referent of the part the *secondary* referent.

3. Pronouns, e.g., "this", "that", "I", "he", "she", and "it".
4. Titles, e.g., "the prime minister", "the pope".

Class 4 hardly deserves separate mention, since it shades off into definite descriptions at one end and proper names at the other.

4.4   *Necessary conditions for referring*

The question I propose to ask regarding these expressions is: What conditions are necessary for the utterance of one of them to constitute a successfully performed categorical definite reference? And as a preliminary to answering this I ask the prior question: What is the point of a definite reference, what function does the propositional act of referring serve in the illocutionary act? And the answer to this, as I have said, is that in definitely referring the speaker picks out or identifies some particular object which he then goes on to say something about, or to ask something about, etc.

But this answer is incomplete for it does not yet state whether or not this identification is conveyed to the hearer. To remove this ambiguity we need to distinguish between a *fully consummated reference* and a *successful reference*. A fully consummated reference is one in which an object is identified unambiguously for the hearer, that is, where the identification is communicated to the hearer. But a reference may be successful—in the sense that we could not accuse the speaker of having failed to refer—even if it does not identify the object unambiguously for the hearer, provided only that the speaker could do so on demand. So far we have been discussing successful references, but it is easy to see that the notion of a fully consummated reference is more basic, for a successful reference is one which if not yet fully consummated is, so to speak, at least potentially so.

In light of this distinction let us rewrite our original question to ask how it is possible that an utterance of an expression can be a *fully consummated reference*. What conditions are necessary for the utterance of an expression to be sufficient to identify for the hearer an object intended by the speaker? After all, it is only *words* that come from the speaker, so how do they identify *things* for the hearer? The way we have formulated the questions will provide us with clues for the answer: Since the speaker is identifying an object to the hearer, there must, in order for this to be successful, exist an object which the speaker is attempting to identify, and the utterance of the expression by the speaker must be sufficient to identify it. These two conditions I have already articulated in a preliminary form as the axiom of existence and the axiom of identification. In the light of our present discussion let us restate them in the form of conditions for a fully consummated reference.

Necessary conditions of a speaker's performing a fully consummated definite reference in the utterance of an expression are:

1. There must exist one and only one object to which the speaker's utterance of the expression applies (a reformulation of the axiom of existence) *and*
2. The hearer must be given sufficient means to identify the object from the speaker's utterance of the expression (a reformulation of the axiom of identification).

Now, let us consider how an utterance of a definite description can satisfy these requirements. Suppose for example that the expression " the man " is uttered as part of the sentence " The man insulted me ". How does such an utterance satisfy our two conditions ?

The first condition may be divided into two parts:

1*a*. There must exist at least one object to which the speaker's utterance of the expression applies.

1*b*. There must exist not more than one object to which the speaker's utterance of the expression applies.[1]

In the case of definite descriptions, the satisfaction of 1*a* is quite simple. Since the expression contains a descriptor and since the descriptor is or contains a descriptive general term, it is only necessary that there should exist at least one object of which the descriptor could be truly predicated. In the case of " the man " it is only necessary that there exist at least one man for condition 1*a* to be satisfied.

The next step is more complex. The temptation of course is to overdraw the parallel between the conditions 1*a* and 1*b* and to assert that just as 1*a* is satisfied if there exists at least one object of which the descriptor could be truly predicated, so 1*b* is satisfied if there exists at most one object of which the descriptor is true. This temptation is particularly strong if one regards a successful definite reference as a kind of disguised assertion of a true uniquely existential proposition, i.e., a proposition asserting the existence of one and only one object satisfying a certain description. Such a view is taken by Russell in the theory of descriptions. Analyzed according to the theory of descriptions an utterance of the above sentence would have to be construed as asserting the existence of only one man in the universe.

Does this criticism seem disingenuous? Of course it is as it stands, for Russell did not have in mind contexts like the above when he formulated the theory. But however disingenuous, it is far from pointless, for notice how he excludes such contexts: he says that in the contexts to which the theory is supposed to be applied the definite article is used " strictly so as to imply uniqueness ".[2] But what is the force of " strictly " in this disclaimer ? There

---

[1] The word " apply " here is deliberately neutral and hence, I fear, inadvertently vague. If the reader objects to it—and I have hesitations about it myself—read instead of " to which the speaker's utterance of the expression applies ", " to which the speaker intends to refer in his utterance of the expression " and *mutatis mutandis* throughout. What I am trying to get at is how noises identify objects. One thing that has to be cleared up is what it is to intend or mean a particular object. But nothing in my argument hinges on the vagueness of the term " apply ".

[2] *Principia Mathematica* (Cambridge, 1925), vol. I, p. 30.

is nothing loose or unstrict in the above sentence; it is as literal and strict as any other. Clearly the force of "strictly" so as to imply uniqueness must be either:

(a) strictly so as to indicate that the speaker intends to refer identifyingly to a particular object; *or*

(b) strictly so as to imply that the descriptor which follows is true of only one object.

Now of these two, (a) cannot be what is meant since the example satisfies (a) and thus leaves the theory open to the charge of absurdity which I have just made. But if (b) is what is meant, it is a question-beggingly false account of the "strict" use of the definite article. Not only is it the case that uses of the definite article with a non-unique descriptor are perfectly strict, but there are in fact no uses of the definite article where it is *by itself* sufficient to imply (or in any way indicate) that the descriptor which follows it is true of only one object. There are, of course, uses of the definite article with descriptors true of only one object—and these are of crucial importance in the speech act of definite reference, as is stated by the principle of identification—but it is not part of the force of the article to imply that they are unique. That is not its function. Its function (in the cases we are discussing) is to indicate the speaker's intention to refer uniquely; and the function of the descriptor is to identify, in a particular context, for the hearer the object which the speaker intends to refer in that context. As a rival account of "the", I suggest that in its definite referring use (which is only one of its uses) it is a conventional device indicating the speaker's intention to refer to a single object, not an indication that the descriptor which follows is true of only one object. (It is worth noticing here that certain languages, e.g., Latin and Russian, do not have a definite article but rely on the context and other devices to indicate the speaker's intention to make a definite reference.)[1]

My account does not as yet provide a satisfactory explanation of how the utterance of a definite description like the above satisfies requirement 1*b*. I have so far only said there must be at least one object satisfying the descriptor and that, by means of the definite article, the speaker indicates his intention to identify a particular object. But since the descriptor, being a general term, may be true of many objects, what makes the speaker's utterance

---

[1] The theory of description will be discussed in more detail in chapter 7.

of that expression apply to only one? The obvious, but uninformative answer, is that he *intends* only one of the objects within the range of the descriptor. This answer is uninformative in that it does not make clear what is involved in intending or meaning a particular object. In order to give a complete answer to this question, I shall examine the requirements for satisfying condition 2, and then return to a discussion of 1*b* and of the relation between referring and intending.

4.5 *The principle of identification*

The second condition (a formulation of the axiom of identification) requires that the hearer be able to identify the object from the speaker's utterance of the expression. By "identify" here I mean that there should no longer be any doubt or ambiguity about what exactly is being talked about. At the lowest level, questions like "who?", "what?", or "which one?" are answered. Of course at another level these questions are still open: after something has been identified one may still ask "what?" in the sense of "tell me more about it", but one cannot ask "what?" in the sense of "I don't know what you are talking about". Identifying, as I am using the term, just means answering that question. For example, in an utterance of the sentence "The man who robbed me was over six feet tall" I can be said to refer to the man who robbed me, even though in one sense of "identify" I may not be able to identify the man who robbed me. I may not be able, e.g., to pick him out of a police line-up or say anything more about him. Still, assuming one and only one man robbed me, I do succeed in making an identifying reference in an utterance of the above sentence.

We have seen that in the case of a definite description such as "the man" the speaker provides an indication that he intends to refer to a particular object, and he supplies a descriptor which he assumes will be sufficient to identify for the hearer which object he intends to refer to in the particular context of his utterance. Even though the descriptor may be true of many objects, the speaker assumes that its utterance in that context will be sufficient to identify the one he means. If it is in fact sufficient then condition 2 is satisfied. But suppose it is not sufficient. Suppose the hearer does not yet know which man is being referred to. In such a case the question "who?", "what?", "which?" are still in order, and I am arguing that it is a necessary condition of a fully consummated definite reference that the speaker provide an unambiguous answer to these questions. If the speaker has not uttered an expression which answers such questions, then he has not identified an object for the hearer, hence has not consummated the reference, for unambiguous answers to these questions are what constitutes identifying, and identifying is a necessary condition of a fully consummated definite reference.

But of what sorts of answers do these questions admit? At the extremes the answers fall into two groups: demonstrative presentations, e.g., "that—over there," and descriptions in purely general terms which are true of the object uniquely, e.g., "the first man to run a mile in under 3 minutes, 53 seconds." Both the pure demonstrative and the pure description are limiting cases; and in practice most identifications rely on a mixture of demonstrative devices and descriptive predicates, e.g., "the man *we* saw *yesterday*", or on some other form of secondary referent, which in turn the speaker must be able to identify, e.g., "the author of *Waverley*", "the capital of *Denmark*". Furthermore, the speaker must be able to supplement the pure demonstratives, "this" and "that", with some descriptive general term, for when the speaker points in the direction of a physical object and says "this", it may not be unambiguously clear whether he is pointing to the color, the shape, the object and its immediate surroundings, the center of the object, etc. But these kinds of identifying expressions—demonstrative presentation, unique description, mixed demonstrative and descriptive identification—exhaust the field. So identification, and hence satisfaction of condition 2, rests squarely on the speaker's ability to supply an expression of one of these kinds, which is satisfied uniquely by the object to which he intends to refer. I shall hereafter call any such expression an *identifying description*. We may then sum up our discussion of condition 2 by saying that though a speaker may satisfy it even if he does not utter an identifying description, given a suitable context and appropriate knowledge on the part of the hearer, he can only *guarantee* that it will be satisfied if his expression is, or is supplemented with, an identifying description. And since in the utterance of any referring expression he commits himself to identifying one and only one object, he commits himself to providing one of these on demand.

The principle of identification

We are now in a position to resume our discussion of condition 1 b. We left off at the point where the condition that there must not be more than one object satisfying the utterance of an expression appeared to imply that there must have been only one object to which the speaker intended to refer in uttering the expression. And the temptation at this point is to think that this is all that needs to be said about condition 1 b, that the speaker's intention to refer to a particular object is independent of his ability to satisfy condition 2, his ability to identify the object for the hearer. He knows what he means all right, even if he cannot explain it to anyone! But I wish to argue that the two requirements, of uniqueness of intention and ability to identify, are at root identical. For what is it to *mean* or *intend* a particular object to the exclusion of all others? Some facts incline us to think that it is a movement of the soul—but can I intend just one particular object independent of any description or other form of identification I could make of it? And if so, what makes my intention an intention directed at just *that* object and not at some other? Clearly the notion of what it is to intend to refer to a particular object forces us back on the notion of identification by description, and we can now generalize this condition as follows: A necessary condition of a speaker's intending to refer to a particular object in the utterance of an expression is the speaker's ability to provide an identifying description of that object. Thus, the satisfaction of condition 1 b and the ability to satisfy condition 2 are the same. Each requires the speaker's utterance to be, or to be supplementable by, an identifying description.

In other words, the axiom of identification (in its original formulation) is a corollary to the axiom of existence (in its revised formulation). For a necessary condition of there being one and only one object to which the speaker's utterance of an expression applies, one and only one object to which he intends to refer, is that he should be able[1] to identify that object. The axiom of identification follows from the axiom of existence, and—as soon as certain considerations about *the means* of identification are adduced—the principle of identification follows from either.

Furthermore, as I hinted briefly in chapter 1, the principle of identification is a special case of the principle of expressibility.

[1] I assume here and throughout that input and output conditions are satisfied. The fact that a speaker might be unable to satisfy a condition because, e.g., his jaw is paralyzed is irrelevant.

Put crudely, the principle of expressibility says: whatever can be meant can be said. Applied to the present case of definite reference that amounts to saying that whenever it is true that a speaker *means* a particular object (in this case, "means" = "intends to refer to") it must also be true that he can say exactly which object it is that he means. But this is simply a somewhat crude re-formulation of the principle of identification, for the principle of identification only states that a necessary condition of definite reference is the ability to provide an identifying description, and it is the identifying description which provides the vehicle for *saying* what is *meant* in the reference. And it is worth re-emphasizing here that a limiting case of *saying* is *saying* which involves *showing*; that is, a limiting case of satisfying the principle of identification and hence the principle of expressibility is indexical presentation of the object referred to.

In the systematic study of language, as in any systematic study, one of our aims is to reduce the maximum amount of data to the minimum number of principles.

Given our definitions of fully consummated and successful reference and our arguments to show that the ability fully to consummate a reference depends on the ability to provide an identifying description, we can now state (with qualifications to emerge later) the principle of identification as follows:

> 3 *b*. A necessary condition for the successful performance of a definite reference in the utterance of an expression is that either the expression must be an identifying description or the speaker must be able to produce an identifying description on demand.

4.6 *Qualifications to the principle of identification*

The principle of identification emphasizes the connection between definite reference and the speaker's ability to provide an identifying description of the object referred to. By now, this connection must be rather obvious: since the point of definite reference is to identify one object to the exclusion of all others, and since such an identification can only be guaranteed by an identifying description, the conclusion follows. But though this theoretical point seems to me unimpeachable, it will require a certain amount of qualification and explanation to show how it operates in the use of natural languages.

1. In ordinary discourse the hearer may demand no identifying description at all and may simply rest content with the use of a non-identifying expression. Suppose a speaker utters a proper name, say, "Jones". Discourse may proceed even if no identifying description is provided, the hearer assuming that the speaker could produce one on demand. The hearer may, himself, use the name "Jones" to refer in, e.g., asking a question about Jones. In such a case, the hearer's reference is parasitic on that of the original speaker, for the only identifying description he could provide would be "The person referred to by my interlocutor as "Jones"". Such an expression is not a genuine identifying description, for whether or not it does identify depends on whether or not the original speaker has an independent identifying description which is *not* of this form. I shall touch on this problem again in chapter 7, where I attempt to apply the conclusions of this chapter to proper names.

2. Even when the hearer does ask for identification, he may be satisfied with a non-unique descriptor, and communication is not necessarily hampered thereby. To extend the above example, suppose the hearer asks: "Who is Jones?", a non-identifying reply such as, e.g., "an Air Force lieutenant" may provide sufficient identification for the discourse to proceed, but even in such cases the hearer must always assume the speaker could distinguish Jones from other Air Force lieutenants. We might wish to introduce the notion of a *partially consummated reference* to describe such cases. Success in identification may be a matter of degree.

3. Sometimes the descriptor may not even be true of the object referred to and yet the reference is successful. Whitehead offers a good example: speaker, "That criminal is your friend", hearer, "He is my friend and you are insulting".[1] In such a case the hearer knows quite well who is being referred to, but the referring expression, far from being an identifying description, contains a descriptor which is not even true of the object. How does this square with the principle of identification? If we are not careful, such examples are likely to fool us into supposing that there must be much more to referring than just providing identification, that referring must involve a special mental act or at least that every successful reference pre-supposes, besides an existential statement,

[1] Alfred North Whitehead, *The Concept of Nature* (Cambridge, 1920), p. 10.

an identity statement: "The object described by the descriptor is identical with just the one *I mean*". But all this would be incorrect. In the above example there is nothing mysterious, it is clear that the context is sufficient to provide an identifying description, for the word "that" in "that criminal" indicates that the object either is present or has already been referred to by some other referring expression and that the present reference is parasitic on the earlier. The descriptor "criminal" is not essential to the identification, and though false it does not destroy the identification, which is achieved by other means.

One often hears questionable descriptors tacked onto otherwise satisfactory referring expressions for rhetorical effect. In, e.g., "our glorious leader" the word "glorious" is irrelevant to the speech act of definite reference—unless there are several leaders, some of whom are not glorious.

4. It needs to be re-emphasized that in a limiting case the only 'identifying description' a speaker could provide would be to indicate recognition of the object on sight. Children, for example, often learn proper names before any other expressions, and the only test we have of their correctly using the name is their ability to indicate recognition of the object when presented with it. They are unable to satisfy the principle of identification except in the presence of the object.

Such facts should not lead us to think of referring as a wholly unsophisticated act: a dog may be trained to bark only in the presence of its master, but he is not thereby *referring* to his master when he barks—even though we might use his bark as a means of identifying his master.[1]

5. Not all identifying descriptions are of equal usefulness for identification. If I say, e.g., "The Senator from Montana wishes to become President", the referring expression in this sentence may be more useful for identification than if I had said, "The only man in Montana with 8432 hairs on his head wishes to become President", even though the latter satisfies the formal requirements of the principle of identification and the former does not, there being two senators from Montana. Why is this so? Part of the force of the principle of identification is that a reference performed

---

[1] What is the difference? Part of the difference is that a speaker, unlike the dog, intends his utterance to identify by means of getting the hearer to recognize this intention (cf. my discussion of meaning in section 2.6).

in the utterance of a definite description succeeds in virtue of the fact that the expression indicates characteristics of the object referred to; but since the point of definite reference is to *identify* rather than to *describe* the object, the expression best serves its purpose if the characteristics indicated are important to the identity of the object referred to, and important to the speaker and the hearer in the context of the discussion; and not all identifying descriptions are of equal usefulness in these respects. In the last analysis, of course, what is important is what we consider to be important, and it is easy to imagine situations where the number of hairs on a man's head could be of central importance—if, for example, it were regarded by a tribe as having religious significance. In such circumstances people might keep themselves much better informed about the number of everybody's hairs than about their jobs, and in the above examples the latter referring expression might be more useful than the former. The point I wish to emphasize at present, however, is that it is possible for an expression to satisfy the formal requirements of the principle of identification, i.e., to be an identifying description, and still fail to be a useful referring expression. A use of such an expression may still be met with the question "who ("what" or "which") are you talking about?" and it is this question which a definite reference is designed to answer.

4.7 *Some consequences of the principle of identification*

In sections 4.4 and 4.5 I tried to establish the principle of identification and to show the relationship between the axiom of identification and the axiom of existence. Now I propose to develop some of the consequences of the principle of identification. I shall try to do this in a stepwise fashion so that the reasoning will be quite clear, all the assumptions will be out in the open, and any mistakes will be easier to detect. Let us start with the axiom of identification.

1. If a speaker refers to an object then he identifies, or is able on demand to identify, that object apart from all others for the hearer. From this point together with certain considerations about language, it follows that

2. If a speaker refers to an object in the utterance of an expression then that expression must either

(*a*) contain descriptive terms true uniquely of the object,

(*b*) present it demonstratively, or

(*c*) provide some combination of demonstrative presentation or description sufficient to identify it alone.

Or, if the expression is not one of these three, the speaker must be prepared to substitute one of them on demand (principle of identification).

3. In every case, reference is in virtue of facts about the object that are known to the speaker, facts which hold uniquely of the object referred to, and the utterance of a referring expression serves to consummate the reference because and only because it indicates those facts, communicates them to the hearer. This is what Frege was getting at, rather crudely, when he pointed out that a referring expression must have a sense. In some sense a referring expression must have a 'meaning', a descriptive content, in order for a speaker to succeed in referring when he utters it; for unless its utterance succeeds in communicating a fact, a true proposition, from the speaker to the hearer, the reference is not fully consummated. We might put it in this Fregean way: meaning is prior to reference; reference is in virtue of meaning. It follows directly from the principle of identification that every utterance of a referring expression, if the reference is consummated, must communicate a true proposition, a fact, to the hearer. (And this, as we have already seen, is an instance of the principle of expressibility which we discussed in chapter 1.)

4. We need to distinguish, as Frege failed to do, the sense of a referring expression from the proposition communicated by its utterance. The sense of such an expression is given by the descriptive general terms contained in or implied by that expression; but in many cases the sense of the expression is not by itself sufficient to communicate a proposition, rather the utterance of the expression *in a certain context* communicates a proposition. Thus, for example, in an utterance of "the man" the only descriptive content carried by the *expression* is given by the simple term "man", but if the reference is consummated the speaker must have communicated a uniquely existential proposition (or fact), e.g., "There is one and only one man on the speaker's left by the window in the field of vision of the speaker and the hearer". By thus distinguishing the sense of an expression from the proposition communicated by its utterance we are enabled to see how two utterances of the

same expression with the same sense can refer to two different objects. "The man" can be used to refer to many men, but it is not thereby homonymous.

5. The view that there could be a class of logically proper names, i.e., expressions whose very meaning is the object to which they are used to refer, is false. It isn't that there just do not happen to be any such expressions: there could not be any such expressions, for if the utterance of the expressions communicated no descriptive content, then there could be no way of establishing a connection between the expression and the object. What makes *this* expression refer to *that* object? Similarly the view that proper names are "unmeaning marks",[1] that they have 'denotation' but not 'connotation', must be at a fundamental level wrong. More of this in chapter 7.

6. It is misleading, if not downright false, to construe the facts which one must possess in order to refer as always facts *about* the object referred to, for that suggests that they are facts about some *independently* identified object. In satisfying the principle of identification existential propositions play the crucial role, for the possibility of satisfying the principle of identification by giving an identification a non-existential form, e.g., "the man who such and such", depends on the truth of an existential proposition of the form, "there is one and only one man who such and such". One might say: underlying our conception of any particular object is a true, uniquely existential proposition.

The traditional road to substance is taken as soon as one construes facts as always in some sense *about* objects, as soon as one fails to see the primacy of the existential proposition. Wittgenstein made such an irreducible metaphysical distinction between facts and objects in the *Tractatus* when[2] he said that objects could be named independently of facts and facts were combinations of objects. Part of the aim of this chapter is to show that a language conforming to his theory is impossible: objects cannot be named independently of facts.

Thus, the traditional metaphysical notion of an irreducible distinction between facts and objects seems confused. *To have the*

---

[1] J. S. Mill, *A System of Logic* (London and Colchester, 1949), book 1, chapter 2, para. 5.

[2] E.g., 2.01, 3.202, 3.203, 3.21, etc. L. Wittgenstein, *Tractatus Logico-Philosophicus* (London, 1961).

notion of a particular object is just to be in possession of a true uniquely existential proposition, i.e., a fact of a certain kind.

7. Quantification is somewhat misleading in this matter, for it is tempting to regard the bound variable in a proposition of the form $(\exists x)$ (fx) as 'ranging over' previously identified objects, to suppose that what an existential proposition states is that some one or more objects within a range of *already identified* or identifiable objects has such and such a characteristic. To avoid these misleading metaphysical suggestions, propositions of the form $(\exists x)$ (fx) might also be read as "The predicate f has at least one instance", instead of the usual "Some object is f".

8. For these reasons reference is—in one sense of "logical"—of no *logical* interest whatsoever. For each proposition containing a reference we can substitute an existential proposition which has the same truth conditions as the original. This, it seems to me, is the real discovery behind the theory of descriptions. This is not to say, of course, that all singular terms are eliminable or that there is no difference between the original proposition and its revised existential formulation. It is only to say that the circumstances in which the one is true are identical with the circumstances in which the other is true.

4.8 *Rules of reference*

We are now in a position to construct an analysis of the propositional act of reference parallel to our analysis of the illocutionary act of promising in chapter 3. I shall follow the same pattern as there employed of first stating the analysis in terms of conditions and then extracting from those conditions a set of rules for the use of the referring expression. It needs to be emphasized that we are again constructing an idealized model.

Given that S utters an expression R in the presence of H in a context C then in the literal utterance of R, S successfully and nondefectively performs the speech act of singular identifying reference if and only if the following conditions 1–7 obtain:

1. *Normal input and output conditions obtain.*

2. *The utterance of R occurs as part of the utterance of some sentence (or similar stretch of discourse) T.*

3. *The utterance of T is the (purported) performance of an illocutionary act* The act may be unsuccessful. I may succeed in referring to something even though my utterance as a whole is muddled, but the

utterance cannot be absolute gibberish: I must at least be purporting to perform some illocutionary act or other.[1]

4. *There exists some object X such that either R contains an identifying description of X or S is able to supplement R with an identifying description of X.*

This condition captures both the axiom of existence and the principle of identification in accordance with our analysis of sections 4.4 and 4.5.

5. *S intends that the utterance of R will pick out or identify X to H.*

6. *S intends that the utterance of R will identify X to H by means of H's recognition of S's intention to identify X and he intends this recognition to be achieved by means of H's knowledge of the rules governing R and his awareness of C.*

This Gricean condition enables us to distinguish referring to an object from other ways of calling attention to it. For example, I may call my hearer's attention to an object by throwing it at him, or hitting him over the head with it. But such cases are not in general cases of referring, because the intended effect is not achieved by recognition on his part of my intentions.

7. *The semantical rules governing R are such that it is correctly uttered in T in C if and only if conditions 1–6 obtain.*[2]

The reader may find this analysis puzzling as it stands, for at least the following reason. Since the analysis is of reference in general, and is therefore neutral as between reference using a proper name, a definite description or whatnot, it has an extremely abstract character which the analysis of promising managed to avoid. The rules which follow will share that abstract character, that is, they will state what is common to all expressions used for singular identifying reference. The reader should bear in mind that in a natural language like English particular rules will either attach to elements in the deep structure of the sentence or more likely to some product of the combinatorial operations of the semantic component. There is, incidentally, now a certain amount of syntactical evidence to indicate that in the deep structure of English sentences noun phrases are not as diverse as the surface structure

---

[1] This is the speech act reflection of Frege's dictum "Nur im Zusammenhang eines Satzes bedeuten die Wörter etwas". Cf. chapter 2, above p. 25.

[2] The use of the biconditional may seem to be carrying idealization too far. What about e.g. the occurence of R in an existential sentence, where it does not refer? We have to assume that the qualifying "in T" will eliminate such cases.

makes them seem. In particular, some recent research tends to suggest that all English pronouns are forms of the definite article in the deep structure of sentences.[1]

The semantical rules for the use of any expression R to make singular definite reference are:

Rule 1. R is to be uttered only in the context of a sentence (or some similar stretch of discourse) the utterance of which could be the performance of some illocutionary act. (This rule embodies conditions 2 and 3.)

Rule 2. R is to be uttered only if there exists an object X such that either R contains an identifying description of X or S is able to supplement R with an identifying description of X, and such that, in the utterance of R, S intends to pick out or identify X to H.

This is rather an omnibus rule, but I find it most convenient to state as one rule, for there must be one and the same object which exists, to which the expression applies, and which the speaker intends to pick out for the hearer. This rule, extracted from conditions 4 and 5, states that the axiom of existence and the principle of identification apply to every referring expression, as well as making it clear that reference is an intentional act.

Rule 3. The utterance of R counts as the identification or picking out of X to (or for) H.

Notice that, like other systems containing essential rules, these rules are ordered: 2 only applies if the previous rule 1 is satisfied, and 3 only applies if 1 and 2 are satisfied.

---

[1] P. Postal, 'On so-called pronouns in English', mimeo, Queen's College, N.Y.

Chapter 5

PREDICATION

In this chapter we shall attempt to complete our characterization of the illocutionary act by giving an analysis of the propositional act of predication. Predication, like reference, is an ancient (and difficult) topic in philosophy, and before attempting to give a speech act analysis of predication I shall consider certain well known theories of predication and the problems of "ontological commitment" with which they are related. I begin with Frege's account.

5.1 *Frege on concept and object*[1]

In a statement made using the sentence "Sam is drunk" what if anything stands to "—is drunk" as Sam stands to "Sam"? Or is this an improper question? Frege, who assumed it was a proper question, gave the following answer. Just as "Sam" has a sense and in virtue of the sense has a referent namely Sam, so "—is drunk" has a sense and in virtue of that sense has a referent. But what is the referent of "—is drunk"? To this Frege's answer is: "a concept". To which one's natural response would be: "which concept?" And to this the tempting answer is, "the concept *drunkenness* ". But clearly, as Frege sees, this answer will not do, for on that account "Sam is drunk" must be translatable or at any rate must have the same truth value as "Sam the concept drunkenness", in accordance with a version of the axiom of identity which Frege accepts, that whenever two expressions refer to the same object one can be substituted for the other in a sentence without changing the truth value of the corresponding statement. (This is sometimes called Leibniz's law.) But the latter sentence far from being in any sense a translation of the former is either sheer nonsense or simply a list. Hence what is referred to by "—is drunk" cannot be the same as what is referred to by "the concept drunken-

---

[1] Frege's theory of concepts is a part of his overall theory of functions. In what follows, I am confining my remarks to his theory of concepts, although I think the conclusions can be applied generally to his theory of functions.

ness". Thus, either "—is drunk" *does not* refer to the concept in question, or if it does then "the concept *drunkenness*" cannot refer to it as well. Oddly enough Frege opts for the latter solution: He says, e.g., "the concept *horse* is not a concept"; it is an object.[1] Apparently this is a contradiction, but Frege regards it as no more than a mere inconvenience of language.

Contrary to Frege I shall argue that it is not an inconvenience of language but is a muddle arising out of his equivocation with the word "concept". If we give a single meaning to the word "concept" it would be a genuine contradiction. But Frege gave two meanings, and once this equivocation is recognized, and certain distinctions which Frege overlooked are marked, the apparent contradiction can be removed like a diseased member without doing any serious damage to the rest of this part of Frege's theory. I shall commence by analyzing the reasoning by which he arrived at the apparent contradiction.

The apparent contradiction arises because Frege is moving in two philosophical directions which are at bottom inconsistent. He wishes (*a*) to extend the sense-reference distinction to predicates, i.e., to insist that predicates have a referent; and at the same time (*b*) to account for the distinction *in function* between referring expressions and predicate expressions. He uses the word "concept" to mark the results of both tendencies (*a*) and (*b*) and therein is the source of the contradiction, since the two arguments lead to different and inconsistent conclusions. I shall try to make this clear.

Why does Frege move in direction (*a*), that is, why does he say that predicates have referents? The actual texts in which he discusses predication are very unclear about his reasons, but if one considers this problem in the light of his overall philosophical objectives it seems that the desire to extend the sense-reference distinction to predicates is not a mere product of fascination with an analytic tool, the distinction between sense and reference, but arises out of a fundamental necessity of his theory of arithmetic— the need to quantify over properties. He appears to think that the use of a predicate expression commits one to the existence of a property. And if the use of a predicate expression commits one to the existence of a property, does it not follow that in the utterance

[1] P. Geach and M. Black (eds.), *Translations from the Philosophical Writings of Gottlob Frege* (Oxford, 1960), p. 46.

of that expression one refers to a property?[1] Some of Frege's followers,[2] though not Frege himself, present this argument in the following form:

1. Suppose Sam and Bob are both drunk.
2. Then it follows that *there is something* which Sam and Bob both are. Alternatively, *there is* some property which Sam and Bob both have.
3. Therefore in 1, the expression "—are...drunk" refers; it refers to that property which Sam and Bob both have. Let us call this a concept.

Let us call this argument (*a*) and its conclusion, conclusion (*a*). What is wrong with this argument? It contains an obvious *non sequitur*: 3 does not follow from 1 and 2. From the fact that a statement I utter commits me to the existence of a property it *does not follow* that in that statement I *referred* to a property.

In spite of the general agreement among Frege's followers and interpreters that he did rely on some version of argument (*a*), it seems to me not at all clear that he did in fact. But it does seem quite clear that, for whatever reasons, he did accept conclusion (*a*). For he says both that a concept is "the reference of a grammatical predicate"[3] and "I call the concepts under which an object falls its properties".[4] But together with his other views, these imply that predicate expressions refer to properties. Conclusion (*a*) is inconsistent with a separate argument which he clearly does use, as I shall now attempt to show.

Argument (*b*) centers around Frege's insistence that the concept is "predicative", and his insistence on the distinction between the function of a referring expression (*Eigenname*) and the function of a grammatical predicate. This difference in function he marks by a type distinction between objects, which can never be referred to by predicates, and concepts, which he says are "essentially predicative". He grants that this notion of concepts cannot be properly *defined*, but he hopes to *explain* it both by giving us examples of the use of predicative expressions and by certain metaphorical descriptions which he gives of concepts in saying

---

[1] This interpretation is quite common, cf. M. Dummett, 'Frege on functions', *Philosophical Review* (1955), p. 99; H. Sluga, 'On sense', *Proceedings of the Aristotelian Society* (1964), n. 6, p. 31.

[2] E.g., P. Geach, 'Class and concept', *Philosophical Review* (1955), p. 562.

[3] Geach and Black (eds.), *op. cit.* p. 43 n.   [4] Ibid. p. 51.

that they are "incomplete" in contrast with objects which are "complete", and that they are "unsaturated" relative to objects. His successors have found these metaphors both mystifying[1] and illuminating.[2] In any case, Dummett[3] reports that in his later years Frege himself grew dissatisfied with them. I personally find them helpful auxiliaries to understanding the distinction in function between "Sam" and "is drunk" in the assertion "Sam is drunk". But it does not seem to me that we are going to understand the distinction Frege is trying to make until we make a few needed distinctions of our own. Let us distinguish between:

1. A predicate expression.
2. A property.
3. The use of a predicate expression to ascribe a property.

Now, all the arguments, metaphors, etc., which I am calling argument (*b*) concern not 2 but 3, the use of a predicate expression to ascribe a property. That is, on argument (*b*) the thesis, "a grammatical predicate refers to a concept", is equivalent to "a grammatical predicate ascribes a property" (remember that "ascribe" here is meant to carry no assertive force), hence the expression "refers to a concept" just means "ascribes a property". Reference to a concept simply is the ascription of a property. On argument (*b*) the question, "What role does a grammatical predicate play?" is answered equivalently by: it ascribes a property, and by: it refers to a concept (in both cases, of course, it also expresses a sense). Notice on this use of "concept" it does not, so to speak, factor out. There is no sentence beginning, "A concept is..." which will answer the question "What is a concept?" except for such answers as "A concept is the reference of a grammatical predicate". It is this impossibility of factoring out the notion of a concept which leads Frege to say such things as that concepts are incomplete and unsaturated.

This analysis clarifies the type distinction between concepts and objects. For Frege an object is anything that can be referred to by a singular noun phrase, whether it is a property, a particular, a number or whatnot. But reference to a concept just is the ascription of a property in the use of a grammatical predicate.

---

[1] Cf. M. Black, 'Frege on Functions', *Problems of Analysis* (London, 1954).

[2] Cf. e.g., Geach, *op. cit.*

[3] Unpublished report to Lit. Hum. Board, Oxford, 1955.

And now the origin of the apparent contradiction is obvious. In conclusion (*a*), Frege used "concept" to mean "property", and hence, "refer to a concept" means "refer to a property". In argument (*b*), "refer to a concept" means "ascribe a property in the use of a grammatical predicate". He uses the word "concept" in these two inconsistent ways in almost the same breath: "I call the concepts under which an object falls its properties"; "the behaviour of the concept is essentially predicative".[1] It is clear that these two remarks are inconsistent, for the properties of an object are not essentially predicative: they can be referred to by singular noun phrases as well as ascribed to an object in the utterance of predicate expressions. Thus two different meanings are given to "concept" and at once an apparent contradiction ensues. "The concept *horse* is not a concept." The concept horse, i.e. a *property*, is clearly what, according to conclusion (*a*), "is a horse" refers to; but reference to it cannot be reference to a concept, i.e. *the ascription of a property*, as alleged by argument (*b*). The reference of "the concept horse" cannot be the same as the reference of a grammatical predicate, because "the concept *horse*", though a possible grammatical subject, cannot be a grammatical predicate.

Since we have seen argument (*a*) to be invalid anyway and since we have discovered two quite distinct meanings of "concept", let us scrap the term "concept" and try to say what Frege was saying in a different terminology. Frege's statement "the concept *horse* is not a concept" simply means: "the property of horseness is not itself an ascription of a property"; or to put it even more clearly in the formal mode: "the expression "the property horseness" is not used to ascribe a property, rather it is used to refer to a property". And on this interpretation Frege's contradiction is changed into an obvious truth.

But of course Frege could not have adopted my proposed solution because of conclusion (*a*). He seems to have thought that in order to quantify over properties he had to insist that predicate expressions *referred* to properties. Thus, on this view, a concept simply is a property. But at the same time, since he recognized the nature of the distinction between reference and predication, he tried to make reference to a property do the job of predication, and the only way he could do this was to equivocate with the word "concept". That entity which is referred to by a predicate ex-

---

[1] Geach and Black (eds.), *op. cit.* p. 51 and p. 50 respectively.

pression is not, as first appeared, a property, but is an entity such that reference to it just is the ascription of a property to an object. Hence the apparent contradiction.

But, to repeat, once the impulse to insist that predicate expressions must *refer* is removed, all the problems dissolve. The distinction between reference and predication holds, and the correct description is to say that the predicate expression is used to ascribe a property. I do not claim that this description has any *explanatory* power at all. Nobody who does not already have a prior understanding of what it is to use a predicate expression can understand this remark, as we shall shortly see (in section 5.5). At this stage I only claim that it is literally true and that it reproduces the element of Frege's account which survives after the contradiction-producing mistake is removed.

The removal of the false view that predicate expressions refer to properties in no way prejudices the possibility of quantification over properties. It only appeared to because quantification on argument (*a*) appeared to entail reference, and hence to deny reference, by contraposition, appeared to involve a denial of quantification.

It might be thought that the difficulties I have posed for the Fregean theory of predication rest merely on certain inconvenient usages of English and similar languages, and that if we were to make certain revisions my objections would collapse. It does seem to me, however, that these objections are valid regardless of changes one might care to make in the language, and since the view that predicates refer is fairly widespread[1] it may be worthwhile to state in a general form the arguments against it.

If one is given two premises, which all the philosophers in question hold implicitly or explicitly, one can derive a *reductio ad absurdum* of the thesis that it is the function of predicates to refer. The premises are:

1. The paradigmatic cases of reference are the uses of singular referring expressions to refer to their referents.
2. Leibniz's law: if two expressions refer to the same object they are intersubstitutable *salva veritate*.

Combine these with the thesis:

3. It is the function of predicate expressions, like singular referring expressions, to refer.

---

[1] Cf. e.g., R. Carnap, *Foundations of Logic and Mathematics* (Chicago, 1939), p. 9.

Then in any subject–predicate proposition of the form "fa" arbitrarily assign any proper name "b" to the referent of the predicate, and by substitution we can reduce the original sentence to a list: "b a", which is not even a sentence.

At this point there are two possible maneuvers. One can say:

(*a*) The sense of "refer" (and hence of "stand for", "designate", and all the rest) is different for predicates from what it is for singular referring expressions. Hence the reduction to a list is invalid.

(*b*) The entity referred to by the predicate is a very peculiar entity, so peculiar indeed that as soon as we try to refer to it with a referring expression (*Eigenname*) we find ourselves referring to an entity of a different kind. Hence it is impossible to assign a name to it, and the reduction to a list is invalid.

Frege in effect adopted (*b*). Neither of these attempts to avoid the breakdown is satisfactory. Maneuver (*a*) leaves the notion of referring in the case of predicates wholly unexplicated and amounts in effect to a surrender of the thesis at issue, since in the statement of the thesis the relation of a singular referring expression to its referent was presented as the paradigm of referring. Maneuver (*b*) again is surrounded by mystery and incomprehensibility, and apart from that it produces a formal contradiction as soon as we apply a general term to the kind of thing which is referred to by the predicate—a contradiction of the form, e.g., the concept *horse* is not a concept.

Alterations in languages do not seem to me to be able to avoid these consequences, and for these reasons I believe that the notion that some entity stands to a predicate as an object stands to a singular referring expression should be abandoned.

But, quite apart from the question of whether or not predicates refer, is it possible to justify quantification over properties? Do universals exist?

5.2 *Nominalism and the existence of universals*

Nominalism nowadays usually takes the form of a refusal to 'countenance' or 'quantify over' entities other than particulars, of refusing to undertake any 'ontological commitments' to non-particular entities. Universals, as one kind of non-particular, come under this general nominalist ban. But before assessing the nominalist objection to universals, one wants to know what exactly the nature of a commitment to universals is. How exactly am I committed if, for example, from the fact that Sam is bald, I infer that there is something Sam is, and from that, that there is some property, namely baldness, which he has, and that, therefore, baldness exists. What am I saying when I allow baldness into my ontology? It will not do simply to announce that I am platonizing, violating Ockham's razor, pretending to comprehend incomprehensible entities, and generally removing myself from those more ascetic philosophers who 'eschew' universals, for one would like to know how much these charges amount to.

To answer this question let us first ask: if two people, who agree that Sam is bald, disagree over whether or not to introduce baldness into their ontology, what kind of disagreement are they having? It is not in any sense a factual disagreement since the person who inferred his conclusion on the basis that Sam is bald could have drawn the same conclusion from the statement that Sam is not bald. No alteration in the facts in the world affects his conclusion. (In this respect the philosopher's use of these sentences sometimes differs from the ordinary use of sentences like "baldness exists", for in at least one ordinary use an assertion using this sentence would be equivalent to asserting that at least one thing is bald.) In short, for the sort of realism or platonism that is here under discussion, the statement that a given universal exists is derivable from the assertion that the corresponding general term is meaningful. Any meaningful general term can generate tautologies, e.g., "either something or nothing is bald" and from such tautologies, the existence of the corresponding universal can be derived. Thus the dispute about whether or not to quantify over universals, on at least one interpretation, is a pseudo-dispute, because the force of the quantifier is simply to assert that which both sides agree on, that the predicate is meaningful.

But, it might be objected, is not this just begging the question in favor of realism? Is not the realist–nominalist dispute (in at least one of its many forms) precisely a dispute over the question of whether the existence of universals can be so derived? As an answer to this question consider examples of the sorts discussed earlier. As far as the ordinary meanings of these statements are concerned (and when we talk about these entailments it is those meanings that we are talking about), the statement that Sam and

Bob are both intelligent does indeed entail the statement that there is something that they both are, namely intelligent, and another way of making that statement is to say that they both have the quality (attribute, characteristic, property) of intelligence, from which follows the statement that there is at least one quality that they both have. But by a similar argument, from the statement that neither of them is intelligent, it follows that there is at least one quality they both lack. Of course, realists have talked a great deal of nonsense about universals, and universals do readily lend themselves to nonsensical talk (e.g., where are they, can you see them, how much do they weigh? etc.) if we take them on the model of our material object paradigms of thinghood. But the fact that it is possible to talk nonsense does not disqualify the above derivations as specimens of valid reasoning conducted in ordinary English.

Insofar as the nominalist is claiming that the existence of particulars depends on facts in the world and the existence of universals merely on the meaning of words, he is quite correct. But he lapses into confusion and needless error if his discovery leads him to deny such trivially true things as that there is such a property as the property of being red and that centaurhood exists. For to assert these need commit one to no more than that certain predicates have a meaning. Why should one wish to avoid such ontological commitments if they commit us to no more than we are already committed to by holding such obvious truths as that e.g., the expression "is a centaur" is meaningful? Of course, the nominalist may well have been confused by the dust raised by his platonic opponents: he may e.g. be unable to understand what Frege meant in alleging the existence of a "third realm" of entities, or he may object to platonistic theses which commit us to facts of which he may be doubtful such as e.g., the theory of mathematics which insists that in order for there to be an infinite series of natural numbers there must be an infinite number of particulars. But platonism need not take such forms, and the nominalist is confused if he rejects it in those forms where it is obviously and harmlessly true.

There is a perfectly general point here which can be stated as follows: if two philosophers agree on the truth of a tautology, such as e.g. "everything coloured is either red or not red", and from this one concludes that the property of being red exists, and the other refuses to draw this conclusion; there is and can be no dispute, only a failure to understand. Either they mean something different by the derived proposition or, counter to hypothesis, they do not understand the original proposition in the same way. There are no other possibilities. But if they agree that the first is a tautology then there can be no commitment undertaken by the second which is not undertaken by the first, and since tautologies commit us to no extralinguistic facts, there is no factual commitment in the second. From tautologies only tautologies follow.

In general, one may say that if one wishes to know what one is committed to when one asserts that an entity exists, one should examine the grounds which are advanced to prove its existence. (This is merely a special case of the dictum: to know what a proof proves look at the proof.)

I believe that much of the emptiness which surrounds the discussion of these issues comes from a neglect of this principle, as we shall see in the next section.

5.3 *Ontological commitments*

In this section I wish to explore further the notion of an ontological commitment, at least as it has occurred in recent philosophizing.

Some philosophers, notably Quine, have been attracted by the view that there could be a criterion of ontological commitment, a criterion which would enable one to tell what entities a theory was committed to. In an early work Quine states this criterion in terms of the variables of the quantification calculus. "To be assumed as an entity is, purely and simply, to be reckoned as the value of a variable."[1] More recently this view is expressed as follows:

> Insofar as we adhere to this notation [of quantification], the objects we are to be understood to admit are precisely the objects which we reckon to the universe of values over which the bound variables of quantification are to be considered to range.[2]

I find this criterion extremely puzzling and indeed I am puzzled by much of the recent discussion concerning ontological commitments, and my conclusion, toward which I shall now argue, is

[1] W. Quine, *From a Logical Point of View* (Cambridge, 1961), p. 13.
[2] W. Quine, *Word and Object* (Cambridge, 1960), p. 242.

that there is no substance to the criterion and indeed very little to the entire issue. Let us begin by considering an alternative criterion.

Criterion 2. A theory is committed to those entities and only those entities which the theory says exists.

Someone might, as a start, object to this criterion on the grounds of the vagueness of "says". Sometimes a theory might not explicitly say that a certain entity exists but nonetheless it might imply or entail that the entity exists. So I shall revise it as follows:

Criterion 3. A theory is ontologically committed to those entities and only those entities which the theory says or entails exist.[1]

But it will be objected that this criterion is trivial. To which the answer is that it is trivial, but nonetheless any non-trivial criterion must give exactly the same results as this trivial criterion. It is a condition of adequacy of any non-trivial criterion that its output satisfy the trivial criterion. What then is the point of having a non-trivial criterion? Well, a non-trivial criterion such as Quine's might provide us with an *objective* test or criterion of ontological commitment. Criterion 3 relies on such notions as entailment; and there are notorious disputes about what is and what is not entailed by a theory; but Quine's criterion, it might be argued, gives us an objective way of settling such disputes. If our interlocutor is willing to express his theory in the "canonical notation" of quantification theory, then by examining the use of the bound variables in his theory we can objectively decide what entities the theory is committed to. But there is something very puzzling about this suggestion because of the following consideration: sometimes a statement couched in one notational form can involve a commitment which, in some intuitively plausible sense, is exactly the same as the commitment involved in a statement couched in quite a different notational form. By way of commitment there may be nothing to choose between them. Furthermore, there may be no paraphrasing out procedure that determines that one is more primitive, or is preferable to the other. Yet on the criterion the two statements, though they involve the same commitments in fact, would involve different commitments.

An argument of this form has been proposed by William Alston[2] and I summarize what I take to be the tendency of the discussion, beginning with Quine's position.

---

[1] Cf. A. Church, 'Ontological commitment', *Journal of Philosophy* (1958).
[2] W. P. Alston, 'Ontological commitment', *Philosophical Studies*, vol. 9 (1958) pp.8–17.

As it is unlikely that I shall be able to reproduce exactly the thoughts of the real Quine and Alston, I shall discuss the views of two imaginary philosophers Q and A.

Q: We can eliminate apparent commitments to unwelcome entities by paraphrase into a notation which makes explicit our real ontological commitments. For example, the apparent commitment to the existence of miles which occurs in the statement, "There are four miles between Nauplion and Tolon", can be eliminated with the formulation: "Distance in miles between Nauplion and Tolon = four."[1]

A: There is no commitment in the first which is not in the second. How could there be? The second is just a paraphrase of the first, so if the first commits you to the existence of miles so does the second. A man's existential commitments depend on the statements he makes, not on the sentences he uses to make them.

Q: A's objection misses the point. By paraphrasing into the notation of the second we prove that the commitment in the first was apparent and not necessary. It is not that the first clearly contains a commitment which is not contained in the second but rather that it appears to contain such a commitment and by paraphrasing the original we show that this was merely an appearance. The advantage of the criterion is that it allows us to become clear as to the exact extent of our commitments. The criterion is itself ontologically neutral as between different commitments. Besides, the paraphrase makes no synonymy claims. We don't care if it says exactly the same (whatever that means) as the statement which it paraphrases.

A: This discussion is extremely puzzling. On Q's criterion it looks as if any statement can be paraphrased into equivalent but notationally different statements which according to the criterion would give different results, even though the commitments were the same. Consider the commitment "At least one chair exists", i.e. 1. $(\exists x) (x$ is a chair$)$. Now paraphrase that in the form "The property of chairhood has at least one instance", i.e. 2. $(\exists P) (P =$ chairhood and P has at least one instance$)$. On Q's criterion it seems the commitments in these two must be different, but since the second is merely a para-

[1] Cf. W. Quine, *Word and Object*, p. 245.

phrase of the first, it is hard to see how there can be any difference in commitment.

Q: We need only to formulate a reply along the lines of the original reply to A considered above: The commitments to abstract entities in the second of the above two statements are *unnecessary*. There is no need for any such commitment because any sentence like 2 can be paraphrased into a sentence like 1. And is not this just another way of saying that the commitments are only apparent and not real? Or alternatively, if A insists that they are real, then is it not just one of the advantages of explication that we can get rid of them without any cost in usefulness to theory? The criterion shows us that in 1 we are rid of the unwelcome commitments of 2.

A: Q misses the point. There cannot be any commitments in 2 which are not in 1 because exactly the same state of affairs in the world which makes 1 true makes 2 true. The commitment is a commitment to the existence of such a state of affairs, whatever notation you choose to state it in.

I want now to extend A's answer to Q, and to attack the whole notion of a purely objective or notational criterion of ontological commitment by showing that if we really take it seriously we can show that any ontological commitment you like is only apparent simply by paraphrasing it in the spirit of Q's paraphrase of the mile example. I wish to prove that if we try to work with the criterion, ontological commitments become intolerably elusive, because, given notational freedom of paraphrase in the spirit of Q's discussion of the mile example, we can say anything we like and as far as the criterion goes be committed to anything we like.

I shall prove this by proving that as far as the criterion goes we can assert all existing scientific knowledge and still remain committed only to the existence of this pen.[1]

Let "K" be an abbreviation for (the conjuction of statements which state) all existing scientific knowledge.[2]

Define a predicate "P" as follows:

$$P(x) = df. \ x = \text{this pen} \cdot K$$

---

[1] I am indebted to Hilary Putnam for showing me this way of expressing the point. I do not know if he agrees with it.

[2] If someone objects to the notion of "all existing scientific knowledge" as being unintelligible, any reasonably sized fragment of knowledge will do as well, e.g. let "K" abbreviate "There are dogs, cats, and prime numbers".

Proof: 1. This pen = this pen   (axiom)
   2. K (axiom)
   3. ∴ This pen = this pen$\cdot K$
   4. ∴ P (this pen)
   5. ∴ $\exists x(Px)$

Thus, in the spirit of Q's ontological reduction we demonstrate that, in terms of Q's criterion of ontological commitment, the only commitment needed to assert the whole of established scientific truth is a commitment to the existence of this pen.[1] But this is a *reductio ad absurdum* of the criterion. Those statements for which "K" is an abbreviation will contain an enormous number of commitments which would naturally be described as ontological, and any paraphrase such as the above must contain exactly the same commitments as the original. The stipulative definition of "K" guarantees precisely that it contains the same commitments. But according to the criterion of ontological commitment in our canonical notation we can assert all of these commitments without actually being committed to them. Therefore, the use of the criterion in this case involves us in a contradiction, for it is contradictory to assert (*a*) The assertion of all existing scientific knowledge involves us in commitments to the existence of more objects than just this pen (which is obviously true) and (*b*) To assert all existing scientific knowledge involves us only in the commitment to the existence of this pen (which is what we prove using the criterion). Since, therefore, the criterion leads us to contradict obvious facts it must be abandoned as a criterion of ontological commitment.

Notice that it is not an adequate reply to this to say that the statements for which "K" is an abbreviation must be formalized so as to reveal their separate ontological commitments, because the criterion does not determine how a theory is supposed to be formalized. I think that 5 is an absurd formulation of scientific knowledge, but there is nothing in the criterion that excludes it as a statement of theory.

This proof is intended as a *reductio ad absurdum* of the criterion for those with a nominalistic bias. An even simpler proof could be formulated for someone with a platonistic bias.

---

[1] Notice that 5, the statement of the 'theory', satisfies Q's condition of being in canonical notation, that is, it employs only quantificational logic and predicates.

Let "q" be the proper name of the proposition which is formed by the conjunction of all known true propositions.[1] Then all knowledge can be symbolized as follows (letting "p" range over propositions): $(\exists p)(p = q \cdot p$ is true)

Thus on the criterion the only thing to whose existence we are commited is one proposition.

To these arguments it might be replied that they rest on the notion of synonymy, which Quine rejects. But this reply is inadequate first, and less importantly, because it would make Quine's supposedly neutral criterion of ontological commitment dependent on very controversial views concerning synonymy; secondly, and more importantly, because the only synonymies on which the above proof rests are introduced by explicit stipulation and hence would not be open to Quine's objections even if those objections were really valid.

Someone might make another objection to the first proof on the grounds that 'predicates' such as "P" are incoherent or nonsensical, etc. I do not know how exactly such an objection would proceed, but in any case it is not one which is open to Quine, as he himself uses precisely this sort of device[2] in his discussions of modality. I conclude that Quine's criterion fails as a criterion for ontological commitments. It would indeed have been extremely surprising if it had succeeded for we would then have had the conclusion that notational forms were a sure guide to existential commitments, and it seems impossible that that should be the case. To paraphrase Alston, it is what a man says, not how he says it, that commits him.

But if that is the case we may wonder if the notion of an onto-logical commitment in general is as clear as we originally supposed. The moral of this discussion seems to be that there is no such thing as a class of irreducibly existential or ontological commitments. Anything which is said in the form of an existential sentence can be rephrased in some other form. And it is no answer to that to say paraphrases make no synonymy claim, for the point is some para-phrases have exactly the same commitments as the original state-ment paraphrased, because exactly the same state of affairs that would be required to make one true would also be required to

---

[1] It is necessary to treat "q" as a proper name and not as an abbreviation to avoid a variation of the use-mention fallacy.

[2] W. Quine, *From a Logical Point of View* (second edition), pp. 153 ff.

make the other true. Philosophers have, I think, long since given up the idea that there are irreducibly negative sentences; why do they suppose there must be irreducibly existential sentences? Imagine the futility of a criterion for negational commitment (and the related problem of 'deniology').

This being so there seems to be no separate problem of ontological commitments. There is indeed a problem of how we know those facts which our utterances commit us to. Among these will be such as are naturally expressed in an existential form. "Is there life on other planets?" "Do abominable snowmen exist?" The alleged problem of ontology is thus swallowed up in the general problem of knowledge, for notation is no sure guide to commitment. So our trivial criterion 3 (p. 107) of ontological commitment really amounts to saying: A man is committed to the truth of whatever he asserts.[1]

In the previous two sections I have perhaps not yet made it clear that underlying these confusions I am trying to expose there is a more profound confusion: it is to suppose that talk of universals is somehow puzzling or unwelcome or metaphysical, and we would be better off, other things being equal, if we could do without it. But to say "The property of saintliness is something none of us possesses" is just a fancy way of saying "None of us are saints". The really profound mistake is not to see the harmlessness of the first way of saying it.[2]

Let us summarize the conclusions of this chapter so far.

1. Frege was correct in drawing a crucial distinction between the functions of a referring expression and a predicate expression.

2. His *account* results in a contradiction because he wished to claim that a predicate expression also refers. The usual arguments for this claim are invalid, and the claim results in inconsistency with the correct conclusion 1. Hence it must be abandoned.

[1] Incidentally the stilted and sometimes archaic terminology in which these discussions are carried on is a clue that something is fishy. I know how, for example, to eschew tobacco or alcohol, but how do I analogously "eschew" universals? I can countenance or refuse to countenance rude behavior by my children, but how do I go about countenancing numbers or classes? The use of "recognize" is not much better. If someone informs me seriously that he recognizes the existence of material objects, one's feeling is likely to be either, "How could he fail to?" (blindness? amnesia?) or else like that of Carlyle ("He'd better").

[2] Which is not to say that people can't talk nonsense about universals—as they can about anything.

3. The abandonment of this claim does not threaten his account of arithmetic, for it is not tantamount to denying the existence of universals.

4. On at least one interpretation, universals exist, and the proposition that any given universal exists is (or can be stated as) a tautology.

5. Quine's criterion of ontological commitment is unsuccessful.

6. There is no such thing as a class of irreducibly existential commitments.

5.4   *The term theory of propositions*

So far, then, our answer to the question which began our discussion, "What stands to the predicate " —is drunk " as Sam stands to "Sam"?", is "Nothing". But perhaps we are too hasty in drawing this conclusion. Perhaps Frege's failure to find a symmetry of subject and predicate results only from his attempt to discover symmetry in an extreme form, and a symmetrical account can be given, though of a more modest kind.

Strawson[1] has attempted to describe the subject–predicate proposition in terms more neutral than Frege employs, but along Fregean lines. (I do not say he is inspired by Frege.) Strawson says that both subject and predicate identify "non-linguistic items" or "terms" and introduce them into the proposition where they are joined by a "non-relational tie". Thus, e.g., in a statement making use of the sentence "The rose is red", the expression "the rose" identifies a particular, a certain rose, and the expression "is red" identifies a universal, the property of being red, or, for short, redness. In the proposition the universal and the particular are joined by a non-relational tie. Here two weaknesses of Frege's theory of concept and object are avoided. Strawson avoids saying that predicates refer by adopting the (apparently) neutral term "identify", and he avoids saying that a sentence is a list, without involving himself in a contradiction, by appealing to the notion of a non-relational tie. The following diagrams (p. 114) are an attempt to make clear the distinction between Strawson and Frege. I shall, hereafter, refer to the theory in figure 2 as "the term theory".

Is the term theory any more satisfactory than Frege's? It is important to emphasize that Strawson does not regard it, as it stands, as an explanation of the distinction between subject and predicate,

[1] P. F. Strawson, *Individuals* (London, 1959).

but only as a description, one possible description, among others, which will provide us with a neutral terminology for discussing certain philosophical problems. I shall argue that it is a false description and as such bound to distort any discussion of these problems.

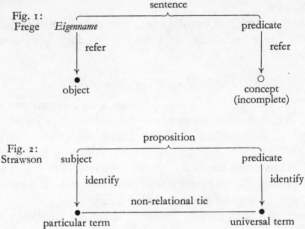

Fig. 1:
Frege

Fig. 2:
Strawson

If one were to approach the term theory in a captious spirit, one might point out that the notion of a non-relational tie, if taken literally, defies explanation. Further, one might point out that to say that a particular is introduced into a proposition, that it occurs in a proposition, must be nonsensical on any literal interpretation. But these captious objections rest on the unsympathetic approach of taking literally expressions intended as metaphors. But not all the expressions are intended as metaphors. We are meant to take literally the remark that both expressions *identify non-linguistic entities*. Let us now scrutinize this remark.

In what sense, exactly, is the term identified by "is red" non-linguistic? It is easy to see in what sense the term identified by the subject expression, "the rose", is non-linguistic, it is a material object, its existence is a contingent fact. But is the universal in any similar sense non-linguistic? In our discussion of nominalism we saw that the existence of a universal followed from the meaning-fulness of the corresponding general term or predicate expression. But is the meaning of the predicate expression a linguistic or a non-linguistic entity? In a perfectly ordinary sense it is a linguistic entity. And can the existence of a non-linguistic entity follow from the existence of a linguistic entity? Either our discussion of nominalism was mistaken or else universals are no more non-linguistic than the meanings of words. For universals, to use an old-fashioned jargon, essence and existence are the same, and that is just another way of saying that (in general) the propositions asserting their existence are (or can be) tautologies. But it cannot be tautologous that any non-linguistic entities exist. Entities such as universals do not lie in the world, but in our mode of representing the world, in language. True, universals are not linguistic in the way that words (considered as phonetic sequences) are, but they are linguistic in the way that meanings of words are, and hence linguistic in the way that words with meanings are.

So on any ordinary criterion for distinguishing linguistic from non-linguistic entities the remark is false. Of course it may be that all that is meant by calling universals non-linguistic is that they are not words (phonemes or graphemes), but on that view a great many things which we ordinarily think of as linguistic become non-linguistic. In any case, the right hand arrow in our diagram (Fig. 2) has no business going outside the proposition, for the left hand arrow points out of the proposition at objects in the world; whereas, to repeat, universals do not lie in the world.

Such considerations might lead us to doubt the helpfulness of the remark that both predicates and subjects identify non-linguistic entities. These doubts will, I think, be increased if we switch our scrutiny from the term "non-linguistic" to the term "identify". We have seen that in a fully consummated reference the speaker identifies an object for the hearer by conveying to the hearer a fact about the object. But in uttering a predicate expression the speaker does not identify a universal in a manner at all analogous. To make this point clear let us examine what it would actually be like to attempt to 'identify' a universal in the way that one identifies a particular. Let us rewrite:

  1. The rose is red

to read:

  2. The rose is the color of the book.

If we suppose the book in question to be red, then 2 will have the same truth value as 1. And here 'identification' of the universal has been done in a way analogous to the way one identifies a particular: by presenting a fact about it. But is there some unitary sense of "identify" in which both 2 and 1 *identify redness*? In answering this question, let us remember that 2 only says:

> 3. The rose and the book are the same color.

And it is, I think, clear that in the sense in which 1 identifies redness, 3 fails to identify redness, for it fails to answer the question *which* color. (Of course, if the hearer already knows the book is red, then he will be able to infer from 2 and 3 that the rose is red. But this does not show that 2 and 3 identify redness in the sense in which 1 does: we need to distinguish what is identified in or by a proposition from what can be inferred from the proposition and additional premises.) The only situation in which the speaker could identify redness in the utterance of a sentence such as 2 would be a situation where an instance of redness is in sight of the speaker and hearer at the time and place of the utterance, a situation in which 2 could be rewritten as:

> 4. The rose is *that* color (accompanied, say, with a pointing gesture at a red book).

With these exceptions, utterances of sentences such as 2 and 3 fail to identify a universal while utterances of a sentence such as 1 succeed. I do not say that there is no sense of "identify" in which 2 and 3 identify redness, only that in the full sense of "identify" in which 1 identifies it they do not.

In other words, the only way we have of identifying particulars in their absence is precisely not a way of fully identifying universals in the absence of any of their instances. Why? To answer this we need only to revert to our discussion of some paragraphs back. Universals are not entities in the world, but in our mode of representing the world; they are, therefore, identified not by appealing to facts in the world, but in the utterance of expressions having the relevant meanings. To put it shortly, we might say that universals are not identified via facts, but via meanings. The only exceptions to this remark are cases where the speaker presents the hearer with an actual instance of the universal, but these cases will not appear too exceptional if we recall that it is just in these cases that the meanings of empirical general terms are learned—they are the ostensive learning situations. So our account amounts to saying that the universal is only identified in the full sense either by presenting the hearer with the relevant meaning (in less metaphysical jargon: uttering a corresponding expression) or by placing him in a situation where the meaning could be learned.

The aim of this discussion has been to show that the term theory employs the expression "identify" in two quite different senses, or, to put it more circumspectly, that the means of identifying universals are quite different from the means of identifying particulars, and that this is a consequence of the fact that universals are parts of our mode of describing the world, not parts of the world.

So far, though, our discussion of "identification" does not present any new objections to the term theory. It does, however, pave the way for a serious objection:

The term theory begins by taking the identification of particulars in the utterance of singular referring expressions as the paradigm of identification. It then weakens, or alters, this sense of "identify" to allow that predicate expressions identify universals. But, as I shall argue, as soon as we adjust our terminology to permit ourselves to say that predicate expressions identify universals, we must, in consistency, say that subject expressions identify universals, in the same sense of "identify" as well. To put the point generally, any argument which will show that the predicate expression identifies a universal must also show that the subject expression identifies a universal. If in 1 "is red" identifies redness, then "rose" identifies the property of being a rose, or, for short, rosehood. If this point is not immediately obvious, remember that we can rewrite 1 as:

5. The thing which is a rose is red.

And this identifies no more and no fewer universals than:

6. The thing which is red is a rose.

I can think of no argument which would show that in either 5 or 6 "is red" identifies a universal which would not also show that "is a rose" identifies a universal. Clearly it will not do to appeal to the notion of "aboutness", because for every context in which one would wish to say 5 is *about* redness, one can find an equally plausible context in which one would wish to say that it was *about* rosehood.

My argument, then, against the term theory is that it stops too soon. It begins by noting that referring expressions identify objects, it then asks, "What do predicate expressions identify?" and comes up, after suitable adjustment in the notion of identifying, with the answer: "universals". But as soon as the adjustments which permit the answer are made, it follows that the subject expression must identify universals as well. So we cannot describe the symmetries and asymmetries of a subject–predicate proposition such as 1 by saying that both expressions identify terms, one a particular, one a universal; for insofar as either term identifies a universal, they both do. Proper names and indexical expressions will not be exceptions for, according to the principle of identification, if their utterances constitute a fully consummated reference, they too must convey to the hearer a proposition, which will have descriptive content and consequently, 'identify universals'.

I conclude, then, that the picture offered by the term theory is a false one. First, because universals are not 'non-linguistic items', and, secondly, because if predicate expressions identify universals, as the theory alleges, then so do subject expressions, as the theory fails to note. If one wished to formulate a correct description of a paradigmatic subject–predicate proposition, employing such intensional notions as properties, concepts and the like, one would have to say, in a Fregean vein, that in the expression of the proposition one expresses a subject concept and one expresses a predicate concept. Neither are non-linguistic entities. In the expression of the subject concept one refers to an object, provided, of course, that there is an object satisfying the concept.

Diagrammatically:

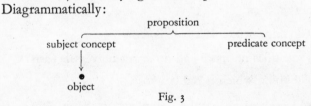

Fig. 3

I do not think this picture is necessary, for I do not think that it is necessary to introduce the notion of concepts, but it is at least correct.

The term theory tries to force a symmetry on this picture first by driving the predicate concept out of the proposition (universals are "non-linguistic items") and secondly by trying to construe the particular as just as much *in* the proposition as the universal (both universals and particulars are "introduced into the proposition"). The result is the incorrect picture in figure 2 above.

The matter might be expressed as follows: the term theory construes predication as a peculiar kind of reference. But if one insists on symmetry, it would be more accurate to construe reference as a peculiar kind of predication: the principle of identification might be regarded as saying that reference is identification via predication. In the utterance of a sentence such as 1, both the subject and the predicate convey to the hearer some descriptive or predicative content. The distinction between subject and predicate is one of function. The subject serves to identify an object, the predicate, if the total illocutionary act is one of describing or characterizing, serves to describe or characterize the object which has been identified. This would be one correct description of the matter.

5.5 Predicates and universals

At this point I wish to make an observation which seems to me essential in understanding the relation of predicate expressions to universals. We have already seen that the existence of any universal follows from the meaningfulness of the corresponding general term. I now wish to extend this to say that in order to have the notion of a certain universal, it is necessary to know the meaning, to be able to use, the corresponding general term (and hence the corresponding predicate expression). That is, to understand *the name of a universal* it is necessary to understand the use of the corresponding general term. But the converse is not the case. "Kindness" is parasitic on "is kind": "is kind" is prior to "kindness". A language could not contain the notion of "kindness" unless it contained an expression having the function of "is kind", but it could contain "is kind" without "kindness".

This priority of predicate expressions over property names is shown by the fact that we could imagine a language capable of making statements (and performing other illocutionary acts) which contained only expressions used to refer to particulars and inflected predicate expressions—but not one which contained only expressions used to refer to particulars and expressions used to refer to properties. We could speak a language containing expressions like "Socrates" and "this rose" along with "is a man", and "is red", but not one which along with the former contained only expressions like "wisdom", "redness". We could not even teach these latter expressions unless our student already understood what it was to be red or to be wise; and to understand these is just to understand the use of the corresponding predicates.

Of course, once we have mastered the use of the predicate expressions, it is easy to derive the corresponding property name. Sometimes we wish to speak about what is common to all things of which a general term is true, and since the paradigmatic device for speaking about is the grammatical form of the referring expressions, it is natural to coin referring expressions such as "wisdom", "kindness", etc. Hence, the hypostatization of such abstract entities, and hence also the harmlessness of the hypostatization as we saw in our discussion of nominalism.

A clue to this dependence of property names on general terms is that property names are almost always cognates of the corresponding general terms: e.g., "wise" generates "wisdom", "kind" generates "kindness", etc. In a syntaxless language there could be no difference and we should have to guess from the context whether or not the expression was used to refer or to predicate. In a language like English, property names are generated by nominalization transformations on underlying phrase markers containing the corresponding predicate expressions. The semantic primacy of the predicate expression is reflected syntactically by its priority in a generative grammar.

Once we see that having the notion of a given universal is parasitic on knowing how to use the corresponding predicate, that, to put it briefly, universals are parasitic on predicate expressions, predicate expressions prior to universals, certain philosophical issues become clear to us. For example, it is obvious that we cannot get any *criteria* for the subject–predicate distinction by appealing to the particular–universal distinction. The term theory might seem to suggest certain such criteria to us, but they would be hopelessly circular since one cannot comprehend the notion of a given universal without first understanding the corresponding predicate expression, and consequently the notion of the universal provides no criterion for the subject–predicate distinction.[1] (I am not here making the *general* point that one cannot have the general notion of "particular" and "universal" without the speech acts of refer-

---

[1] For the contrary view see Strawson, *Individuals*, part 2.

ring and predicating—but the special point that one cannot have the notion of *any given universal* without knowing how to use the general term from which that universal is derived.)

Furthermore, this account of universals explains how the semantic conditions for referring to universals are quite different from the semantic conditions for referring to particulars. In order to satisfy the axiom of identification for particulars, a speaker has to be in possession of a contingent fact as described by the principle of identification. In order to satisfy the analogue of the principle of identification for universals no such factual information is necessary. The axiom of identification for universals requires only that the speaker know the meaning of the general term which underlies the abstract singular term used to refer to the universal.

Again, our insight into the derivative nature of universals provides an easy rationale for the old metaphysical doctrine that only universals, not particulars, can be predicated.[1] I might note in passing that to anyone who holds the term theory such a doctrine might seem to pose a philosophical problem; since the term theory alleges a symmetry of subject and predicate, such asymmetries must seem to require explanation.[2] But once we see the priority of predicates over universals, the doctrine reduces to a grammatical triviality: to say that some speaker "predicated a property" can only mean that he used a predicate expression in the performance of a successful illocutionary act. But then the metaphysical view that one can only predicate properties reduces to saying that only predicate expressions can be predicate expressions. What might have seemed a metaphysical insight reduces to a grammatical tautology.

5.6   Is predication a speech act?

So far the argument of this chapter must seem mainly negative. I have been concerned at some length to cast doubt on the adequacy of two ways of describing singular subject–predicate propositions such as 1 (p. 115). Both these ways have features in common. Both construe the predicate side as analogous to the subject side, and both make the analogy by stating that abstract entities stand to the

---

[1] Aristotle, *Categories*. (I do not say Aristotle would have approved my formulation of this view.)
[2] Strawson attempts to give one, *loc. cit.*

predicate expressions in a way similar to the way concrete entities stand to the subject expressions. I think that this analogy does not hold. I justify devoting so much space to attacking these theories on the grounds that the tendency to construe predication as a kind of, or analogous to, reference is one of the most persistent mistakes in the history of Western philosophy.[1] No effort to eradicate it is too great. And in my view there is no hope of understanding the distinction between reference and predication until it is eradicated.

What then is the nature of the speech act of predication? Let me begin to answer this by saying that predication, in a very important sense in which reference and the various illocutionary acts are speech acts, is not a separate speech act at all. This can be illustrated by considering the following examples, "You are going to leave", "Leave!", "Will you leave?", "I suggest that you leave". An utterance of each of these sentences predicates "leave" of you in a variety of different illocutionary acts. In our canonical notation each is of the form $F\begin{pmatrix} R & P \\ \text{you} & \text{leave} \end{pmatrix}$ where the different values for the variable "F" mark the different illocutionary forces. But now notice an interesting feature of the relation between the various "F's" and the "leave" which does not hold between the "F's" and the "you". The different force indicating devices determine, as it were, the mode in which "leave" is predicated of you. The F term operates on the predicate term so as to determine the mode in which it relates to the object referred to by the referring term: if the sentence is interrogative, its interrogative character (F term) determines that the force of the utterance is to ask whether the predicate (P term) is true of the object referred to by the subject (R term). If the sentence is imperative, its imperative illocutionary force indicating device (F term) determines that the object referred to by the R term is to do the act specified by the P term, and so on through other examples.

In each case, according to this analysis, the illocutionary force indicating device operates on a neutral predicate expression to determine a certain mode in which the question of the truth of the predicate expression is raised *vis-à-vis* the object referred to by the subject expression. Notice on the other hand that the F term does

[1] For a striking example see, e.g., V. Lenin, *Marx–Engels Marxism* (Moscow, 1951), p. 334.

not affect the role of the R term. Its role is always to identify, quite neutrally (even though the sort of object identified may be a function of the *F* term). One might express this difference by saying reference always comes neutrally as to its illocutionary force; predication never comes neutrally but always in one illocutionary mode or another. Even though reference is an abstraction from the total illocutionary act, it is a separate speech act. By analogy, moving the knight is an abstraction from playing chess (because it only counts as moving the knight if you are playing chess), but it is still a separate act. Predication is also an abstraction, but it is not a separate act. It is a slice from the total illocutionary act; just as indicating the illocutionary force is not a separate act, but another slice from the illocutionary act. Why then do we need the notion at all? We need the notion because different illocutionary acts can have a common content, as we saw in our set of examples above, and we need some way to separate our analysis of the illocutionary force aspect of the total illocutionary act from the propositional content aspect. If we remember the senses in which predication (and hence the propositional act) is an abstraction from the total illocutionary act, there is no harm in referring to it as "the speech act of predication". What we are speaking of, though, is that portion of the total illocutionary act which determines the content applied to the object referred to by the subject expression, leaving aside the illocutionary mode in which that content is applied. So the analysis which follows will not parallel the analysis of reference and of illocutionary acts. What we are analyzing is again, as in chapter 3, the illocutionary act, but now we are analyzing that part of it which has to do with the content, in the sense illustrated above.

5.7 *Rules of predication*

Before attempting the analysis there are certain issues that need to be clarified if only briefly. First, I have said that predication presents a certain content, and the mode in which the content is presented is determined by the illocutionary force of the sentence. Is there any way to characterize this presentation which is less metaphorical than the foregoing, but still preserves the abstraction of predication from any particular kind of illocutionary act? The answer to this question, if there is one, will give us the analogue of the essential condition for predication. I can think of no better answer to this question than that which is suggested by the previous paragraph. To predicate an expression " *P* " of an object *R* is to raise the question of the truth of the predicate expression of the object referred to. Thus, in utterances of each of the sentences, " Socrates is wise", "Is Socrates wise?", "Socrates, be wise!" the speaker raises the question of the truth of "wise" of Socrates. This formulation is a bit awkward,[1] but it does have certain advantages. "Raising the question of..." as here construed is not an illocutionary act. Rather, it is what is common to a wide range of illocutionary acts. Thus, to repeat, the man who asserts that Socrates is wise, the man who asks whether he is wise, and the man who requests him to be wise may be said to raise the question of his being wise (of whether "wise" is—or in the case of request will be—true of him). Similarly, one cannot just raise the question and do nothing else. Thus, even if a speaker said "I hereby raise the question of whether Socrates is wise (of Socrates' being wise, of whether "wise" is true of Socrates, etc.)", we would, I think, interpret his utterance as *asking* whether Socrates is wise. One only raises the question in the performance of some illocutionary act or other. Or to put this another way, one cannot just raise the question without raising it in some form or other, interrogative, assertive, promissory, etc. And all this mirrors the fact that predication is not an act which can occur alone, but can only occur as part of some illocutionary act.

This characterization of predication has the merit of explaining certain data which are hard to explain otherwise. For example, philosophers since the publication of Wittgenstein's *Tractatus* have often said that tautological utterances like "Either it's raining or it's not raining" do not say anything or are empty. Nothing could be further from the truth. There is a vast difference between saying of a politician "Either he is a Fascist or he isn't" and saying of him "Either he is a Communist or he isn't". Both of these are tautological assertions but the difference between them is to be explained by the difference in predication. The first raises the question of his being a Fascist, the second raises the question of his being a Communist. The literal illocutionary act of assertion here carries no risk, for the proposition asserted is a tautology, but within the

---

[1] It is especially awkward for imperatives because the aim of imperatives is to get the world to conform to words, whereas "true", when asserted of illocutions, attributes success in getting words to conform to the world.

proposition the very act of predicating such things may be warranted or unwarranted. Such kinds of predication incidentally may introduce new and rather weak kinds of illocutionary force not carried by any illocutionary force indicating device. Thus, e.g., in certain contexts the first might be partly paraphrased as "I suggest that it might be the case that he is a Fascist", which has the illocutionary force of a suggestion. The very act of predication of such an expression may introduce new illocutionary forces.

It is important to emphasize that this use of the verb "predicate" and the cognate noun "predication" is a matter of choice and to that extent arbitrary. In this case, as so often, the very choice of a taxonomy gives a certain direction to the analysis. I have found this taxonomy to work better than others I have tried, but I do not deny that others are possible.

The relation between predication and truth can perhaps be made a bit clearer. To know the meaning of a general term and hence a predicate expression is to know under what conditions it is true or false of a given object. It is true under certain conditions, false under others—and for some objects and some predicates neither true nor false under any conditions, as we shall see. If a speaker asserts a proposition concerning an object, he commits himself to there being the state of affairs in the world in which the predicate is true of the object (and *mutatis mutandis* for other kinds of speech acts). The predicate indicates which state of affairs concerning the object the speaker is committing himself to. The older philosophers were not wrong when they said: to know the meaning of a proposition is to know under what conditions it is true or false. But their account was incomplete, for they did not discuss the different illocutionary acts in which a proposition could occur.

We have throughout the analysis of speech acts been distinguishing between what we might call *content* and *function*. In the total illocutionary act the content is the proposition; the function is the illocutionary force with which the proposition is presented. In the act of identifying reference, the content is the sense of or identifying description associated with the utterance of the referring expression; the function is the role of identifying an object in which that sense is presented. As I have tried to make clear, this distinction does not genuinely apply to predication. Predication provides only content, and the role in which the content is presented, at least in the kinds of simple speech acts we have been considering, is determined entirely by the illocutionary force of the utterance. The characterization of predication in terms of "raising the question" does not specify a separate act, but only what is common to all illocutionary acts in which a given content can occur.

This abstract character of the notion of predicates is bound to raise difficulties for continuing our analysis to cover them; however, we won't know whether the analysis will work or not if we don't try it. So let us consider the following.

Given that *S* utters an expression *P* in the presence of *H*, then in the literal utterance of *P*, *S* successfully and non-defectively predicates *P* of an object *X* if and only if the following conditions 1–8 obtain:

1. *Normal input and output conditions obtain.*

2. *The utterance of P occurs as part of the utterance of some sentence (or similar stretch of discourse) T.*

3. *The utterance of T is the performance or purported performance of an illocutionary act.*

4. *The utterance of T involves a successful reference to X.*

In order for the speaker to predicate an expression of an object, he must have successfully referred to that object.

5. *X is of a type or category such that it is logically possible for P to be true or false of X.*

The object must be of a type or category such that the predicate expression or its negation could be true or false of it. Correlative with the notion of any given predicate is the notion of a category or type of objects of which that predicate could be truly or falsely predicated. For example, correlative with the predicate "is red" is the notion of colored (or colorable) objects. "Is red" can be predicated only of objects which are colored or colorable. We can truly or falsely predicate "red" of windows, but not of prime numbers. We might put this point by saying "is red" *presupposes* "is colored", following Strawson, where "presuppose" is defined contextually as: an expression *a* presupposes an expression *b* if and only if in order for *a* to be true or false of an object *X*, *b* must be true of *X*.[1]

We can then summarize conditions 4 and 5 of predication as follows: For any speaker *S*, any object *X* and any predicate *P*, it is a necessary condition of *S*'s having predicated *P* of *X* in the utter-

[1] Cf. J. R. Searle, 'On determinables and resemblance', *Proceedings of Aristotelian Society*, supplementary vol. (1959), for further discussion of this point.

ance of a sentence containing P, that X should have been successfully referred to in that utterance and all the presuppositions of P
should be true of X.

6. *S intends by the utterance of T to raise the question of the truth or
falsity of P of X* (in a certain illocutionary mode, which mode will
be indicated by the illocutionary force indicating device in the
sentence).

7. *S intends to produce in H the knowledge that the utterance of P
raises the question of the truth or falsity of P of X* (in a certain illocutionary mode), *by means of H's recognition of this intention; and he intends
this recognition to be achieved by means of H's knowledge of the meaning of
P.*

8. *The rules governing P are such that it is correctly uttered in T if and
only if conditions 1–7 obtain.*

Rules for the use of any predicating device P (to predicate P of
an object X):

Rule 1. P is to be uttered only in the context of a sentence or
other stretch of discourse T the utterance of which could be
the performance of some illocutionary act.

Rule 2. P is to be uttered in T only if the utterance of T involves
a successful reference to X.

Rule 3. P is to be uttered only if X is of a type or category such
that it is logically possible for P to be true or false of X.

Rule 4. The utterance of P counts as raising the question of the
truth or falsity of P of X (in a certain illocutionary mode determined by the illocutionary force indicating device of the
sentence).

PART II

Some Applications of the Theory

Chapter 6

THREE FALLACIES IN
CONTEMPORARY PHILOSOPHY

In this chapter I wish to expose three related fallacies in contemporary philosophy, and then, using the concepts and methods of the first part of this book, to offer a diagnosis of them and an alternative explanation of the relevant linguistic data. The three fallacies, as I shall attempt to show, are interrelated and all stem from a common weakness, the failure to base particular linguistic analyses on any coherent general approach to or theory of language. Linguistic philosophers of what might now be called the classical period of linguistic analysis, the period roughly from the end of the Second World War until the early sixties, showed a nice ear for linguistic nuances and distinctions but little or no theoretical machinery for handling the facts of linguistic distinctions once discovered. One of the aims of this work is to provide us with the beginnings of a theory of speech acts. Such a theory if adequate ought to be able to deal with certain kinds of linguistic distinctions in a more adequate way than the *ad hoc* methods of the classical period. This chapter, therefore—in addition to being an exposure of the fallacies—will be both an application of the theory to current philosophical problems and, to the extent that the theory is capable of dealing adequately with these problems, a further confirmation of the theory.

As I am about to make some criticisms of contemporary linguistic philosophy, perhaps this is a good place to remark that I regard the contribution made by this kind of philosophy as truly remarkable. It is only a slight exaggeration to say that it has produced a revolution in philosophy, a revolution of which this book is but one small consequence. The effort I am about to make to correct a few errors should not be taken as a rejection of linguistic analysis.

6.1   *The naturalistic fallacy fallacy*

The first fallacy I shall call the *naturalistic fallacy fallacy*. It is the fallacy of supposing that it is logically impossible for any set of statements of the kind usually called descriptive to entail a statement of the kind usually called evaluative. Linguistic moral philosophers of the classical period made a great deal of the supposed fact that no set of descriptive statements could entail an evaluative statement; and with some, perhaps slight, injustice to Moore they called the belief that such an entailment was possible, the naturalistic fallacy.[1] The view that descriptive statements cannot entail evaluative statements, though relevant to ethics, is not a specifically ethical theory; it is a general theory about the illocutionary forces of utterances of which ethical utterances are only a special case.

The arguments to show that no descriptive statements could entail evaluative statements are not easy to summarize, but fortunately there is a simpler way to refute them than by going step by step through the arguments. The simplest way to show that they are mistaken is to give counter-examples where statements which are clearly cases of what the theorists in question would consider 'descriptive' obviously and unquestionably entail statements which are clearly cases of what the theorists in question would consider 'evaluative'. In order that there be no doubt about whether the examples I present really are examples of what the authors meant by evaluative and descriptive statements respectively, I shall confine my examples to those used by a prominent author from within the group I am discussing. What I intend to do is to show that certain examples which have been presented to illustrate the *impossibility* of deriving evaluative from descriptive statements are precisely examples where the evaluative statements *are derivable* from descriptive statements. I begin with J. O. Urmson's well-known article, 'Some questions concerning validity'.[2]

Urmson says, "I take it that once stated it is obvious that "valid" is an evaluative expression. To speak of a good argument

---

[1] Though I shall continue to use this terminology, it is with some hesitation since the contemporary view is really quite different from Moore's. Cf. *Principia Ethica* (London, 1903), chapter 1. I shall not be concerned with Moore's conception of the "naturalistic fallacy".

[2] *Revue Internationale de Philosophie* (1953); reprinted in A. G. N. Flew (ed.), *Essays in Conceptual Analysis* (London, 1956), pp. 120 ff.

is in most contexts to speak of a valid argument...It seems that any detailed argument on this point would be otiose."[1]

Further, he says "to call an argument valid is not merely to classify it logically, as when we say it is a syllogism or *modus ponens*; it is at least in part to evaluate or appraise it; it is to signify approval of it. Similarly to call an argument invalid is to condemn or reject it."[2] He goes on to claim that because statements asserting an argument to be valid are evaluative it cannot be the case that they are entailed by or equivalent in meaning to any set of statements which are descriptive or "classificatory". There can be no definitions of "valid" in purely descriptive terms because "valid" is an evaluative term, and, similarly, no descriptive statements can entail a statement of the form "This is a valid argument".

This conclusion is illustrated with regard to deductive arguments. The claims here in effect are two. First there can be no definition of the expression "valid deductive argument" in purely descriptive terms, and secondly no description of a deductive argument can entail that it is a valid deductive argument. Both these claims seem to me to be false, and I now wish to offer counter-examples to illustrate their falsity. In the sense of "definition" in which a definition provides a logical equivalence, that is, a set of logically necessary and sufficient conditions, here is a definition of the expression "valid deductive argument":

X is a valid deductive argument $=_{df.} X$ is a deductive argument and the premises of X entail the conclusion of X.

Furthermore, here is a description of an argument which entails that it is a valid deductive argument:

X is a deductive argument in which the premises entail the conclusion.

Someone might claim that "entails" is an evaluative expression (though I do not see how it could be), but in that case we could use any number of other *descriptions* which would be sufficient to entail the *evaluative* statement "X is a valid deductive argument". For example, "The premises are logically sufficient for the conclusion"; "The conclusion follows logically from the premises"; "It is inconsistent to affirm the premises and deny the conclusion", and so on.[1] Such sentences are used to give descriptions of arguments, and any one such description is sufficient to entail the *evaluative* conclusion that the argument is a valid argument. We thus refute the view that no descriptive statement can entail an evaluative one.

It was a fundamental principle of the theory of language that lay behind the naturalistic fallacy fallacy that there was a logical gulf between the meaning of an evaluative expression and the criteria for its application.[2] The trouble with that doctrine in the present instance is that once you have stated that an argument is deductive you have already laid down the criteria for its validity. So even if there were in general a gulf between the meaning of "valid" and the criteria of validity, there can be no gulf between the meaning of "valid deductive argument" and the criteria of validity because the word "deductive" carries deductive criteria with it. To put this point another way, evaluative statements according to the theory could never be completely matters of objective fact, for it is always in principle possible to disagree over the criteria to be employed in making the evaluation. Ultimately one has to choose some criteria and that choice introduces an irreducibly subjective element into any evaluative statement. But in the present case there is no room for such a choice. Once it is settled that such and such is a deductive argument, there is no logical room for choosing some extraneous set of criteria for evaluating or assessing its validity. To characterize it as deductive is to specify deductive criteria for its assessment. It is not a matter of *opinion* that the argument "all men are mortal and Socrates is a man; therefore, Socrates is mortal" is a valid deductive argument.

Let us restate the point. Urmson considers statements of the form, "*X* is a valid deductive argument" as obvious cases of evaluative statements—and probably rightly so since in uttering such a sentence to make such a statement, one would characteristically be evaluating (giving an evaluation of) an argument. The questions this poses for us are two: first, is it possible to give a definition of "valid deductive argument" in descriptive terms; and, secondly, are there any descriptions we could give of an

---

[1] Some of the descriptions one could give raise difficulties concerning the so-called paradoxes of strict implication, but then so does the notion of validity itself, so I am treating the paradoxes as irrelevant to our present concerns.

[2] Cf. R. M. Hare, *The Language of Morals* (Oxford, 1952), chapter 2.

argument which would entail a statement of the form, "X is a valid deductive argument"? My answer to both questions is yes. Using the terms that are characteristically used in describing logical relations, terms such as "analytic", "follows from ", "logically necessary and sufficient", "true", "self-contradictory", etc., you can form any number of definitions of the expression "valid deductive argument" and consequently there are any number of descriptions of an argument X using these terms which will entail an evaluative statement of the form "X is a valid deductive argument". So we have a clear-cut case where so-called descriptive statements entail so-called evaluative ones, and the case is all the more interesting because it is a case which was originally presented to us as an illustration of the *impossibility* of any such entailment.

Once we rid ourselves of the dogma that no set of descriptive statements can entail an evaluative statement other examples are not hard to find. Consider some examples chosen from another well-known article by the same author, "On Grading".[1] Here Urmson considers the relation between grading terms set up by the British Ministry of Agriculture and Fisheries for grading apples and the criteria provided by the Ministry for applying these terms. For example, the Ministry introduces the expression "Extra Fancy Grade" and lays down certain criteria for its application, which I shall, following Urmson, abbreviate as A, B, and C. Now, asks Urmson, what is the relationship between the statement, "This apple is Extra Fancy Grade" and "This apple has characteristics A, B, and C". According to him, the relationship between them cannot be one of entailment because "Extra Fancy Grade" is an evaluative term and "A", "B", and "C" are descriptive terms. The statement "Anything which is A, B, and C is Extra Fancy Grade" cannot be analytic because of the distinction between describing and evaluating. Now I wish to ask if it is really plausible to suppose that "This apple is Extra Fancy Grade" cannot be logically derived from "This apple is A, B, and C". It is worth noticing that the government paper which he quotes is headed "*Definitions* of Quality" (my italics).[2] The Ministry is offering *definitions* and given the definitions they offer, the statement "Any apple which is A, B, and C is Extra Fancy Grade" is as analytic as any

---

[1] 'On Grading', *Logic and Language*, ed. by A. G. N. Flew, second series (New York, 1953).
[2] *Ibid*. p. 166.

other analytic statement. The man who says "These apples are A, B and C" but denies that they are Extra Fancy Grade either does not understand the terms he is using, or he is using them differently from the way they have been defined or he is contradicting himself. And these are precisely marks of there being an entailment relationship between the two statements.

Of course, the characteristic illocutionary force of *the utterance of* "This apple is Extra Fancy Grade" is no doubt quite different from the characteristic illocutionary force of the utterance of "This apple has characteristics A, B, and C". As Urmson remarks, the characteristic force of the first utterance is to grade the apple, the characteristic force of the second is to describe it. But the fact that the two utterances have characteristically different illocutionary forces is not sufficient to show that *the proposition* expressed in the first utterance does not entail *the proposition* expressed in the second. Closely related to this distinction between the proposition expressed in an utterance and the illocutionary force of the utterance is the distinction between the meaning of the sentence and the force of its utterance, and also, I shall argue, the distinction—not identity—between meaning and use. To get a clear picture of the naturalistic fallacy fallacy we shall have to examine some of these distinctions later, but at present I want merely to note that *in this instance* the nature of the fallacy is to infer from the fact that two utterances have different illocutionary forces that the proposition expressed in one cannot entail the proposition expressed in the other.

So once again we find that examples which were presented to illustrate the impossibility of deriving evaluative from descriptive statements are, under close inspection, precisely examples where descriptive statements do entail evaluative ones.

So far I have not attempted to explain the origin and character of the naturalistic fallacy fallacy—but just to expose it. Later I shall speculate as to its origins and attempt to characterize it more fully.

6.2   *The speech act fallacy*

I now turn to a second and related fallacy which I shall call the *speech act fallacy*.

In the classical period of linguistic analysis, philosophers often said things like the following:

Speech act fallacy

The word "good" is used to commend (Hare).[1]

The word "true" is used to endorse or concede statements (Strawson).[2]

The word "know" is used to give guarantees (Austin).[3]

The word "probably" is used to qualify commitments (Toulmin).[4]

Each of these is of the pattern: "The word W is used to perform speech act A." Furthermore, it was generally the case[5] that philosophers who said this sort of thing offered these statements as (at least partial) explications of the meanings of the words: they offered these statements of the form "W is used to perform act A" by way of philosophical explication of the concept W. Notice also that, in so doing, they drew—in most cases explicitly—an analogy between the words they were discussing and the so-called performative verbs. Just as "promise" is used to make promises, and "bet" to make bets, so they argued "good" is used to commend, and "true" is used to endorse, etc.

Let us call this pattern of analysis the *speech act analysis*. Now, there is a condition of adequacy which any analysis of the meaning of a word must meet—and which the speech act analysis fails to meet. Any analysis of the meaning of a word (or morpheme) must be consistent with the fact that the same word (or morpheme) can mean the same thing in all the grammatically different kinds of sentences in which it can occur. Syntactical transformations of sentences do not necessarily enforce changes of meaning on the component words of morphemes of those sentences. The word "true" means or can mean the same thing in interrogatives, indicatives, conditionals, negations, disjunctions, optatives, etc. If it didn't, conversation would be impossible, for "It is true", would not be an answer to the question "Is it true?" if "true" changed its meaning from interrogative to indicative sentences.

This is an obvious condition of adequacy, but the speech act

[1] R. M. Hare, *op. cit.*

[2] 'Truth', *Analysis*, vol. 9, no. 6 (1949); reprinted in Margaret Macdonald (ed.), *Philosophy and Analysis* (Oxford, 1954).

[3] 'Other Minds', *Proceedings of the Aristotelian Society*, supplementary vol. 20 (1946); reprinted in *Logic and Language*, second series (New York, 1953), and elsewhere.

[4] 'Probability', *Proceedings of the Aristotelian Society*, supplementary vol. 24 (1950); reprinted in *Essays in Conceptual Analysis* (London, 1956).

[5] Though not always, Austin in particular is rather cagey about whether his analysis is supposed to give the meaning of "know".

analysis fails to meet it. There are two ways of construing the analysis and on either way it fails to meet this condition of adequacy. The crude way to construe it is to suppose that when the speech act analysts said, "*W* is used to perform act *A*" they meant every literal utterance of the word *W* is a performance of act *A*. If this is what they meant, it is too easily refuted, for even if an utterance of the sentence, "This is good", is a performance of the act of commendation, the utterance of the sentence, "Make this good", is not the performance of the act of commendation; it is the performance of the act of making a request or giving an order. And there are obviously any number of such counter-examples. It is unlikely that the speech act analysts would make a mistake as crude as that, so we must turn to a second, more sophisticated interpretation. Often the speech act analysts qualified their statements of the form, "*W* is used to perform act *A*" by saying that the *primary* use of *W* is to perform act *A*. They were thus not committed to the view that every literal utterance of *W* is a performance of act *A*, but rather that utterances which are not performances of the act have to be explained in terms of utterances which are.

More precisely, to satisfy the condition of adequacy, the speech act analysts do not need to show that every utterance of *W* is a performance of *A*, but rather they need only to show that literal utterances which are not performances of the act *A* stand in a relation to performances of *A* in a way which is purely a function of the way the sentences uttered stand in relation to the standard indicative sentences, in the utterance of which the act is performed. If they are in the past tense, then the act is reported in the past; if they are hypothetical, then the act is hypothesized, etc. They need to show this, in order to show how the word makes the same contribution to each different sentence, while maintaining that the performative use is the primary use.

Now it is clear that the speech act analysis of the performative verbs satisfies this condition.[1] For example, when one says something of the form, "If he promises that *p*, then so and so", one hypothesizes the performance of the act which he performs when he says something of the form, "I promise that *p*". But it is equally clear that the speech act analysis of the other words: "good", "true", "probable", etc. does not satisfy this condition. Consider

[1] It may, of course, be false on other grounds.

the following examples: "If this is good, then we ought to buy it", is not equivalent to "If I commend this, then we ought to buy it". "This used to be good" is not equivalent to "I used to commend this". "I wonder whether this is good" is not equivalent to "I wonder whether I commend this", etc. Similar counter-examples will refute the speech act analyses of "true", "know", "probable", etc.

The statement " W is used to perform act A ", which was arrived at by a study of simple present tense indicative sentences containing W, does not explain the occurrence of W in many kinds of sentences which are not simple present tense indicative sentences. Yet, obviously W means the same in those sentences as it does in the simple present indicatives, so the statement " W is used to perform act A " cannot be an explanation of the meaning of W, even given the more sophisticated interpretation of this statement.

The general nature of the speech act fallacy can be stated as follows, using "good" as our example. *Calling* something good is characteristically praising or commending or recommending it, etc. But it is a fallacy to infer from this that the meaning of "good" is explained by saying it is used to perform the act of commendation. And we demonstrate that it is a fallacy by showing that there are an indefinite number of counter-examples of sentences where "good" has a literal occurrence yet where the literal utterances of the sentences are not performances of the speech act of commendation; nor are the utterances explicable in terms of the way the rest of the sentence relates the utterance to the performance of the speech act of commendation.

The speech act analysts correctly saw that calling something "good" is characteristically commending (or praising, or expressing approval of, etc.) it; but this observation, which might form the starting point of an analysis of the word "good", was treated as if it were itself an analysis. And it is very easy to demonstrate that it is not an adequate analysis by showing all sorts of sentences containing the word "good" utterances of which are not analyzable in terms of commendation (or praise, etc.).

The point I am making here is not just a point about the word "good", but is a completely general point about a pattern of analysis in philosophy. A common pattern of analysis has been to offer explications or at least partial explication of the meanings of certain philosophically important words by making statements of the form, "Word W is used to perform act A". Now, if someone offers an analysis of the meaning of a word, then what he offers must hold true of all literal occurrences of the word where it has that literal meaning, or else it is not an adequate analysis. The speech act analyses of the words we have been considering are not adequate because the words have lots of literal occurrences where the utterances of the words are not related to the performance of the act in the ways they would have to be related in order that the analysis should not have the consequence that the word would have to change its meaning with changes in the various syntactical types of sentences in which it occurs. In particular: (*a*) there are lots of literal occurrences of the words which are not performances of the speech acts, and, more importantly, (*b*) those occurrences are not explicable purely in terms of the way the rest of the sentence relates the word to the performance of the speech act. It is worth repeating that this objection does not hold against the speech act analysis of the performative verbs (or, for that matter, against a speech act analysis of interjections).

So far, I have said only a little about the origin of this fallacy, but I should like to show how it relates to the naturalistic fallacy fallacy. If one supposes that the meaning of a word like "valid" ties it to a particular range of speech acts, such as grading and evaluating, then, since entailment is a matter of meaning, it will seem impossible that words standing for logical relations, which one does not suppose to be tied essentially to the speech acts such as grading or evaluating, could be used to define "valid". And it will also seem impossible that statements containing only expressions of the latter kind could be sufficient to entail the statement that an argument is valid. Generally, if we take "W is used to perform A" as part of the analysis of W, then for any words, X, Y, Z, where we assume neither X nor Y nor Z is used to perform A, it will seem impossible that W should be definable in terms of X, Y, and Z and impossible that statements of the form "A is W" could be entailed by statements of the form "A is X, Y, Z". The speech act fallacy is thus one of the props supporting the naturalistic fallacy fallacy. In part, because they held a mistaken speech act analysis of certain words, the classical linguistic moral philosophers thought certain kinds of logical relations involving these words could not obtain. In my discussion of the speech act fallacy, I tried to show that the analysis was mistaken; and in my discussion of the naturalistic fallacy fallacy, I tried to show that in certain cases at least the logical relations did obtain.

6.3   *The assertion fallacy*

I now turn to the third fallacy, which is closely related to the second and which I shall call *the assertion fallacy*. It is the fallacy of confusing the conditions for the performance of the speech act of assertion with the analysis of the meaning of particular words occurring in certain assertions.

Linguistic philosophers wish to analyze the meaning of such traditionally troublesome concepts as knowledge, memory, or voluntary action. To do this, they look to the *use* of such expressions as "know", "remember", "free", "voluntary", etc. The trouble with this method is that in practice it almost always amounts to asking when we would make assertions of the form, "I know that so and so", or "He remembers such and such", or "He did such and such voluntarily". But then there is no easy way to tell how much their answers to these questions depend on what it is to *make assertions* and how much is due to the concepts the philosopher is trying to analyze.

The philosopher notices that it would be very odd or bizarre to say certain things in certain situations; so he then concludes for that reason that certain concepts are inapplicable to such situations. For example, Wittgenstein points out that under normal conditions, when I have a pain, it would be odd to say, "*I know* I am in pain".[1] Another linguistic philosopher[2] has pointed out that it would be very odd for normal adult Englishmen in ordinary situations to say, "I *remember* my own name", or "I *remember* how to speak English". But they then conclude that these are points about the concepts of knowing and remembering; that these concepts are only applicable under certain conditions. I, on the other hand, shall argue that the reason it would be odd to say such things is that they are too *obvious* to be worth saying. It's obviously true that when I have a pain, I know I have it, and it's equally obvious that I do now remember my own name and also

[1] Ludwig Wittgenstein, *Philosophical Investigations* (New York, 1953), e.g., para. 246.
[2] B. S. Benjamin, 'Remembering', *Mind* (1956); reprinted in Donald F. Gustafson (ed.), *Essays in Philosophical Psychology* (New York, 1964).

remember how to speak English, and the reason it is odd to announce such things under normal circumstances is precisely because they are too obvious to merit announcing.

But before developing this point in terms of conditions for making assertions, I want to consider some other examples of the same fallacy. Ryle says in the *Concept of Mind*[1] that in their most ordinary employment the adjectives "voluntary" and "involuntary" are used as adjectives applying only to actions which ought not to be done. He says, "In this ordinary use, then, it is absurd to discuss whether satisfactory, correct or admirable performances are voluntary or involuntary".[2]

Austin in his article, "A plea for excuses",[3] has a similar and more general thesis. He says that in the *standard* case covered by *any* normal verb *none* of the range of expressions qualifying actions —expressions such as "voluntary", "intentional", "on purpose", "deliberately", etc.—nor any of their negations are in order. "Only if we do the act named in some *special* way or circumstances different from those in which an act is normally done…is a modifying expression called for, or even in order."[4] He summarizes this thesis in the slogan, "No modification without aberration".[5] Unless the action is aberrant, no modifying concept is applicable.

Extending Ryle's point, Austin notices that it would be odd to *say*, in ordinary circumstances, "I bought my car voluntarily", or "I am writing this book of my own free will", and both philosophers therefore conclude that certain conditions are necessary conditions of the applicability of certain concepts. In each case, as in the cases considered earlier, the author claims that a certain concept or range of concepts is inapplicable to a certain state of affairs because that state of affairs fails to satisfy a condition which the author says is a presupposition of the applicability of the concept. Furthermore, the reasons why these philosophers advance these claims are similar in every case. They notice that in normal situations it would be very odd to *say* such things as, "I remember my own name", "I bought my car voluntarily", "I am writing this of my own free will". They notice that it is appropriate to say these things only under certain conditions, so they then infer that those conditions are conditions for the applicability of such con-

---

[1] G. Ryle, *Concept of Mind* (London, 1949).   [2] G. Ryle, *ibid.* p. 69.
[3] Reprinted in *Philosophical Papers* (Oxford, 1961).
[4] *Ibid.* p. 138.   [5] *Ibid.* p. 137.

cepts as *remember*, *voluntary*, *free will*, etc., and consequently that they are part of the analysis of these concepts. They thus tacitly assume that the conditions for successfully (and accurately) making the assertion, e.g., that I remember my own name, or that I am writing this book of my own free will, form part of an analysis of the concepts of remembering or free will.

These assumptions have been important methodological principles behind much contemporary philosophizing. In order to show that they are false, I now want to consider certain other things it would be odd to say. Consider the following sentences: "He is breathing", "He has five fingers on his left hand". Now ask yourself under what conditions it would be appropriate to actually *utter* these sentences, to make the assertions that would be made with these sentences, and I think you will agree that in standard or normal situations it would be very odd to utter either of them. Just as it is only appropriate to say, "He remembers his own name", when there is some reason for supposing, e.g., that he might have forgotten his name, so it is odd to say "He is breathing", unless there is some reason to suppose, e.g., that he might have stopped breathing, or at least that our audience might have supposed that he might have stopped breathing, or for some other reason might have needed to be reminded that he is breathing. Similarly, we would not *say* "He has five fingers on his left hand" unless there is some abnormal feature of the situation, e.g., if he has six fingers on his right hand, or if we wish to free him of suspicion of being the four fingered left-handed murderer.

But do these points (about what it would be appropriate to *say*) have anything at all to do with the analysis of the concepts of breathing or fingers? Let us go over this ground carefully. We can construct a whole series of sentences: "He remembers his own name", "He knows that he is in pain", "He bought his car voluntarily", "He is writing this book of his own free will", "He is breathing", "He has five fingers on his left hand". We find that it is only appropriate to utter these sentences as assertions under certain conditions. Only if the situation is aberrant—to use Austin's term—is it appropriate to *say* these things.

Now what is the explanation of this fact? The authors who consider the first examples maintain that the explanation has to do with the concepts of remembering, voluntariness, free will, etc. It seems implausible to suppose that similar explanations would work for the concepts breathing, or finger; so I wish to offer the following more general explanation: There are standard or normal situations. People normally remember their own names, know whether or not they are in pain, buy their cars voluntarily, write works of philosophy of their own free will, breathe, and have five fingers per hand. In general, it is inappropriate to assert of a particular standard or normal situation that it is standard or normal unless there is some reason for supposing, or for supposing someone might have supposed, etc., that it might have been non-standard or abnormal. For to remark that it is standard is to suggest that its being standard is in some way remarkable, and to imply or suggest that is often, or in general, to imply or suggest that there is some reason for supposing that it might not have been standard or that the audience might have supposed that it might not be standard or at least that the audience might need to be reminded that it is standard. If a speaker describing a situation knows of no reason why anyone might suppose that the situation is non-standard or aberrant or need to be reminded of its standard character, then asserting that it is standard is simply out of order.

The explanation, then, has nothing to do with the analysis of particular words; it lies in explaining what it is to make an assertion. The assertion—for example, that I remember my own name —is just pointless unless the context warrants it in some way. But that pointlessness has nothing to do with the concept of remembering but with the concept of what it is to make an assertion. The general character of the assertion fallacy, then, is to confuse the conditions for making non-defective assertions with the conditions of applicability of certain concepts. The point is not, "No modification without aberration", but "No remark without remarkableness".

What exactly is the nature of the dispute here? Both sides agree on the existence of certain data, data of the form, "It would be odd or impermissible to say such and such". But there is a disagreement about the explanation of the data. I say the data are to be explained in terms of what in general is involved in making an assertion; the view I am attacking says the data are to be explained in terms of the conditions of applicability of certain concepts. So far the only claims I can make for my analysis are greater simplicity, generality, and perhaps plausibility. But I now wish to present actual counter-examples to certain of the other analyses to try to refute them more conclusively.

It is argued that the conditions of applicability, i.e. the pre-suppositions, of certain concepts render certain statements in certain standard conditions neither true nor false. But now notice that the negations or opposites of those statements are not neither true nor false in normal circumstances but simply false. Consider: "He does not now know whether he has a pain", "He does not remember his own name", "He is no longer breathing", "He did not buy his car voluntarily; he was forced to", "He is not writing this book of his own free will; he is being forced to", "He does not have five fingers on his left hand but six", and so on. In standard or normal conditions there is nothing nonsensical about such statements; they are just false, for it is their falsity which renders the situation standard or normal in the relevant respects. But then, if they are false, are not their denials true?

Furthermore, if we get away from very simple examples as we did in the case of the speech act fallacy, we shall see that such concepts are applicable without any conditions of the sort considered. Consider the following examples: "The system of voluntary military recruitment is a total failure in California", "The ability to remember such simple things as one's name and phone number is one of the foundation stones of organized society", "It is more pleasant to do things of one's own free will than to be forced to do them". These sentences contain the words "voluntary", "remember", and "free will", and their utterance would be appropriate without any of the special aberrant conditions the philosophers said were necessary conditions for their applicability. So, just as in the speech act fallacy, the concentration on a few very simple examples of indicative sentences has led to an incorrect analysis.

One might put the point slightly differently. The character of the mistake I am citing is that it confuses conditions of assertability with presuppositions of concepts. Most concepts do indeed have presuppositions which determine the scope of their intelligible applicability. For example, the concept *divisible by seven* is only applicable to (certain kinds of) mathematical entities. For that reason, it is odd to the point of unintelligibility to assert, "The Boer War is divisible by seven". Now it is also odd—in the present normal, non-aberrant context—to assert, "I am writing this book of my own free will". But the fact that such an assertion is odd except in abnormal or aberrant situations is not sufficient to show that aberrance or abnormality is a presupposition of the applicability of the concept of doing something freely or of one's own free will in a way that being a numerical entity is a presupposition of the applicability of the concept *divisible by seven*. Of course, "intention", "belief", "know", etc., like most interesting words, do indeed have a complicated network of presuppositions, but the methods of classical linguistic analysis are not always adequate to sort them out and distinguish them from conditions for making non-defective assertions.

6.4   *The origin of the fallacies: meaning as use*

I now want to offer some remarks by way of explanation of how these fallacies came to be committed. Linguistic philosophers of the period I am discussing had no general theory of language on which to base their particular conceptual analyses. What they had in place of a general theory were a few slogans, the most prominent of which was the slogan, "Meaning Is Use". This slogan embodied the belief that the meaning of a word is not to be found by looking for some associated mental entity in an introspective realm, nor by looking for some entity for which it stands, whether abstract or concrete, mental or physical, particular or general, but rather by carefully examining how the word is actually used in the language. As an escape route from traditional Platonic or empiricist or Tractatus-like theories of meaning, the slogan "Meaning Is Use" was quite beneficial. But as a tool of analysis in its own right, the notion of use is so vague that in part it led to the confusions I have been trying to expose. And here I think is how its vagueness generated or helped to generate these confusions.

A philosopher wishes to analyze a particular concept, say knowledge or memory. Following the slogan he looks to the use of the verbs "know" or "remember". To do this he gets a few sentences almost invariably of very simple present tense indicative kind, and asks himself such questions as under what conditions would he utter those sentences, and what speech act would he be performing when he uttered them. But since he lacks any general theory of meaning or of syntax or of speech acts, how is he to interpret the answers to these questions once he gets them? In the case of the *assertion fallacy*, certain general conditions for the performance of the speech act of assertion were mistakenly attributed to particular words because it was in the investigation into the use of those words that those results turned up. The slogan gave the philosopher no way of distinguishing between the use of the word and the use of the sentence containing it. The slogan thus further engendered the mistaken conviction that because under certain conditions we don't say such and such, in those conditions *it cannot be the case* that such and such. Applying the slogan, "Meaning Is Use", the philosopher asks himself, "Under what conditions would we *say* that we *remember* such and such or that such and such an act was done voluntarily?" But how is he to know that the answer to those questions does not depend as much on *saying* as it does on the concepts of remembering or voluntariness?

The origin of the *speech act fallacy* is quite similar. The linguistic philosopher takes the question, "What does "good" or "know" mean?" to be the same as, "How is "good" or "know" used?" and confines his discussion to a few simple sentences containing these words. He then finds that in the utterance of those sentences we perform certain speech acts. The slogan, "Meaning Is Use" gives him no way of distinguishing features of the utterance which are due solely to the occurrence of the word he is analyzing from features which are due to other characteristics of the sentences or to other extraneous factors altogether; so he mistakenly concludes that the word "good" by itself is used to perform the speech act of commendation, and having come to that conclusion while examining the so-called *use* of the word "good", he concludes that he has analyzed the meaning of "good", since according to his slogan use and meaning are the same. The transition seems to occur as follows. The philosopher wishes to ask:

1. What does the word W mean?

Since meaning is use, he takes that question to be the same as:

2. How is W used?

which is then tacitly taken to mean:

3. How is W used in simple present tense categorical indicative sentences of the form, e.g., "X is W".

and that is taken to be the same question as:

> 4. How are these sentences containing *W* used?

which is then taken either as:

> 5. What illocutionary act is performed in the utterance of such sentences?

or:

> 6. What are the conditions for the performance of non-defective assertions in the utterance of such sentences? That is, when would we actually say things of the form, "*X* is *W*"?

To assume that answers to 5 necessarily give answers to 1 leads to the speech act fallacy; and to assume that answers to 6 necessarily give answers to 1 leads to the assertion fallacy. Both fallacies stem from assuming 1 means the same as 2.

The origin of the *naturalistic fallacy fallacy* is more complicated, but even it—in some of its more current versions—is in part due to the slogan, "Meaning Is Use". Linguistic philosophers of the classical period were much impressed by the fact that certain indicative sentences were not used to describe states of affairs but were used to give evaluations, assessments, ratings, judgments, rankings, etc. Now seeing that the *use*, in this sense of illocutionary force of the utterance of the sentences, was different from the use or illocutionary force of the utterance of certain descriptive sentences, they concluded that the meaning must be such that no set of descriptive statements could entail an evaluative one. But that conclusion does not follow, for from the fact that the point or illocutionary force of uttering a sentence is 'evaluative' it does not, follow that the proposition expressed cannot be entailed by a proposition expressed in the utterance of a sentence the illocutionary force or point of uttering which would be 'descriptive'. The truth conditions of the one proposition may be sufficient for the truth conditions of the other—even though the point of uttering one sentence may be different from the point of uttering the other sentence. The truth conditions of a proposition have been confused with the point or force of uttering a sentence, because the word "use" is so vague as to include both the truth conditions of the proposition expressed and the point or illocutionary force of uttering the corresponding sentence.

As a tool of analysis, the use theory of meaning can provide us only with certain data, i.e., raw material for philosophical analysis; e.g., that in uttering a sentence of the form, "*X* is good", one is characteristically praising something, or that the sentence, "I remember my own name", is uttered only under certain conditions and not others. How such data are systematically analyzed, explained, or accounted for will depend on what other views or theories about language we bring to bear on such data, for the use theory does not by itself provide us with the tools for such an analysis and can, indeed (as I have tried to show), engender confusions.

6.5 *Alternative explanations*

Now let us see to what extent our theory of speech acts will solve these problems. The theory should be able to provide linguistic explanations for the linguistic characterizations of the classical linguistic analysts, and the explanations should not be open to the sort of objections we made to their explanations.

The case of the assertion fallacy is the easiest, so I will consider it first. We saw in our analysis of the illocutionary act that among the preparatory conditions for many kinds of acts is a condition which gives point or purpose to the act in the total speech situation. In the case of the information bearing class of illocutionary acts (reports, descriptions, assertions, etc.), the condition takes the form that it must not be too obviously the case to both S and H that p—if the assertion that p is to be non-defective. Furthermore, since S always implies the satisfaction of the preparatory conditions in the performance of any illocutionary act, in the performance of any of the information bearing acts S implies a lack of obviousness.

Now the data we need to explain are contained in characterizations such as that it is odd to say, "I *remember* my own name", "I bought my car *voluntarily*", or "I am writing this *of my own free will*", unless the situation is aberrant in some way, and also that when one says, "I remember my own name", etc., one implies that the situation is odd or aberrant.

The theory accounts for the data as follows. Since it is generally obvious that people remember their own names, buy cars voluntarily, and write books of their own free will, etc., the assertion in any given case will be defective, unless the context is odd in a way which calls the obviousness of these things into question. Similarly, the assertion of any one of these propositions will imply that the proposition is not taken as obviously known to be true, and hence, will imply that the situation is odd, since it is only in somewhat odd situations that they would not be obviously known to be true.

I must re-emphasize that my remarks here are not intended to offer any general account of the conditions of applicability of these concepts. I am not saying that "voluntary", "free will", etc., have no presuppositions, that any action at all can intelligibly be characterized as voluntary. On the contrary, I think that action-modifying concepts have a rather complicated network of presuppositions. Furthermore, some of these concepts are, in my view, excluders.[1] "Voluntary", in particular, seems to be an excluder. It gets its meaning by contrast with "under duress", "forced", "compelled", etc. To make matters even more complicated, some of these modifiers are built into the meaning of certain action verbs. Thus, for example, "He volunteered voluntarily", is (at best) pleonastic, and, "He volunteered involuntarily", is self-contradictory (this example was suggested to me by Gilbert Ryle). In short, any account of the occurrences of these words in utterances—even if confined to sentences used to make simple assertions—would have to include not only (*a*) conditions for assertion, but also (*b*) presuppositions, (*c*) the excluder element, (*d*) the fact that these notions form part of the definition of some verbs, and perhaps other features as well. I am only attempting to show here that Austin's general statement—no modification without aberration—is in error, that other instances of the same assertion fallacy—such as Ryle's—are in error, and that their data are better accounted for by my general theory of speech acts.

The data that we have to explain which led to the speech act fallacy are of these sorts: Calling something "good" is characteristically praising, or commending, or recommending, or expressing approval of the thing so called. Furthermore, this seems not to be just a contingent fact, as is shown by the fact that the word "good" itself is sometimes described as a term of praise. Similarly, saying of a statement that it is true is characteristically endorsing, conceding, granting it, or the like. How can it be the case in these and other instances both that calling something *W* is indeed performing

---

[1] Cf. Roland Hall, 'Excluders', *Analysis*, vol. 20 (1959); reprinted in Charles E. Caton (ed.), *Philosophy and Ordinary Language* (Urbana, 1963), for a more complete explication of this notion.

a speech act *A*, and yet it does not explain the meaning of *W* to say *W* is used to perform act *A* ? To put the question slightly differently, using "good" as an example, how can a theory of language such as the one I am espousing explain how the word "good" makes a contribution to the meaning of indicative sentences which is such that calling something good is, as a matter of conceptual truth, characteristically praising, etc., it without falling into the speech act fallacy? A similar question can be posed about "true", "know", etc.

To answer this question regarding "good", first I wish to distinguish between two classes of illocutionary verbs: in group *X*, I include such verbs as "grade", "evaluate", "assess", "judge", "rate", "rank", and "appraise". In group *Y*, I include such verbs as "commend", "praise", "laud", "extol", "express approval", "express satisfaction", and "recommend". These two classes are sometimes lumped together, but I think it is clear that they are different. I may evaluate something favourably or unfavourably, but I cannot extol it unfavourably. I may grade it as excellent or bad, but I cannot praise it as bad. Members of group *Y* thus stand to members of group *X* in a relation something like the relation of determinate to determinable. To praise something is often or perhaps even characteristically to offer an assessment of it. But not just any kind of assessment; it must be a favourable assessment. Not all assessments are favourable.

Now for the purpose of performing acts in the determinable range—assessing, grading, etc.—there is, depending on the subject matter, a range of terms one can use. Thus, e.g., in grading students, we use the latters "*A*", "*B*", "*C*", "*D*", and "*F*". One of the most common of these grading labels—as Urmson calls them —is "good". Other common grading labels are "excellent", "bad", "fair", "poor", and "indifferent". Giving an assessment will characteristically involve (among other things) assigning a grading label; and, conversely, assigning one of these will characteristically be giving an assessment, evaluation, or the like. And the term assigned will indicate the kind of assessment made— favourable or unfavourable, high or low, and so on.

The reason that it is a non-contingent fact that calling something "good" is commending it, or the like, is this: to call it "good" is to assign it a rank in the scale of assessment or evaluation, but to assign it a rank in this scale is just to assess or evaluate it; it is to give a particular kind of evaluation of it. In the case of "good" it is to give it a (fairly) high or favourable evaluation. But giving a high evaluation is characteristically (as I have already suggested) commending or praising or the like—the situation in which the utterance is made determining which of these it is.

So the quasi-necessary truth that calling something "good" is commending it does not tell us the meaning of "good" but tells us about the way the word is embedded in the institutions of group X and the relations between those institutions and the speech acts in group Y. The connection between the meaning of "good" and the performance of the speech act of commendation, or the like, though a necessary one, is thus a connection at one remove.

Well, what does "good" mean anyway? A complete answer to this question is beyond the scope of this discussion. As Wittgenstein suggested, "good", like "game", has a family of meanings. Prominent among them is this one: "meets the criteria or standards of assessment or evaluation". Other members of the family are: "satisfies certain interests", "satisfies certain needs", and "fulfills certain purposes". (These are not unrelated; that we have the criteria of assessment we do will depend on such things as our needs and interests.)

The speech act analysis correctly notes that *saying* that something meets the criteria or standards of evaluation or assessment is giving an evaluation or assessment of a certain kind, namely commendatory. But the incorrect inference that the meaning of "good" is, therefore, somehow explicable in terms of commendation prevents us from seeing what I have been trying to emphasize, that "good" means the same whether I am expressing a doubt as to whether something is good, or asking if it is good, or saying that it is good. For that reason the question, "What is it to call something good?" is a different question from, "What is the meaning of "good"?"

This conclusion, it seems to me, is further borne out if we consider words which have uses rather similar to "good" and which contain the relevant illocutionary-act concepts as morphological constituents. I am thinking of such word as "praiseworthy", "laudable", and "commendable". To call something praiseworthy is characteristically to praise it. But saying on this basis that "praiseworthy" is used to praise does not give us the meaning or explicate the word "praiseworthy". It only tells us that asserting that something is praiseworthy is performing a certain kind of illocutionary act. But that is a *consequence* of the fact that "praiseworthy" means what it does, i.e., "worthy of praise"; it is not an explication of that meaning. The connection between "praiseworthy" and the speech act of praising is not at all like the connection between the verb "to praise" and the speech act of praising. "Good", I am arguing, is like "praiseworthy" and not like "to praise".

Let us now consider how one would deal with the word "true" along these lines. The problem is this: how can it be the case both that—as the speech act analysis notes—calling something true is somehow characteristically endorsing it, conceding it, confirming it, granting it, or the like, and yet that these remarks do not solve or dissolve what Strawson calls "the philosophical problem of truth"? The answer, I suggest, might be along the following lines. We characteristically call something true, as Strawson observes, only if a comment, remark, assertion, statement, or hypothesis, or the like, has already been made or is at least in some way under consideration; in short, only if a proposition is already in the offing. If your house is on fire, I do not rush up to you and announce, "It is true that your house is one fire"; rather, I simply say, "Your house is on fire". The former locution I use only when the proposition that your house is on fire is already under consideration, where the question has already been raised prior to my announcement. But, if this is so, then my announcement involving the word "true" will serve to indicate not only that your house is on fire, but also that the question has been previously raised, and my *affirming* (as opposed to denying) that the proposition is true will serve to indicate that I am in agreement with, or conceding, or endorsing, some other speaker's speech act, the speech act in which he initially raised the question. That is, because we characteristically use the word "true" only when a proposition is already under consideration, and because a proposition is characteristically put under consideration by the performance of some such illocutionary act as asserting, stating, or hypothesizing—because of these two facts—calling something true will place us in a certain relation to that initial illocutionary act (a relation, for example, of agreement or endorsement and conversely in the case of "not true" a relation of disagreement). All of this tells us what sorts of illocutionary acts we might be performing (among others) when we utter the sentence, for example, "It is true that your house is on fire". But for reasons already stated, it still does not tell us the solution to the philosophical problem of truth. These two examples should suffice to show that it is possible to account for the kind of data which formed the basis of the speech act fallacy while avoiding the errors of that analysis.

The naturalistic fallacy fallacy also leaves us a residual problem which I now want to attack. How can it be the case both that descriptive statements can entail evaluative statements and yet the illocutionary forces are different? Isn't this a violation of the fundamental principle that there can't be more in the conclusion of a deductive argument than there is in the premisses? To explain this, we have to introduce a distinction between meaning and use in one sense of "meaning" and one sense of "use". Let us illustrate this in terms of the apple example. The meaning of "Extra Fancy Grade" as a technical term in apple grading is given by the definition in the Ministry of Agriculture and Fisheries table of definitions.[1] Using our abbreviation, "A certain kind of apple is Extra Fancy Grade" means "A certain kind of apple has properties A, B, and C". But of course the use of the term "Extra Fancy Grade" is likely to be quite different from the use of the 'descriptive' expressions, "A, B, and C", precisely because the term "Extra Fancy Grade" was introduced so that apple sorters would have a special term for use in grading apples. Philosophers sometimes talk as if the only purpose for introducing a new term by stipulative definition is to have an 'abbreviation', but this is clearly false; abbreviation is only one motive among many for stipulative definition. "Extra Fancy Grade" means "A, B, and C", but it is not just an abbreviation. So the distinction between meaning and use here involves a distinction between truth conditions on the one hand and purpose or function on the other. The reason the statement that this apple is A, B, and C, entails the statement that this apple is Extra Fancy Grade, and yet the characteristic illocutionary force of an utterance of the sentence used to make the second statement is to grade and the characteristic illocutionary force of an utterance of the sentence used to make the first statement is to describe, is simply that entailment is a matter of meaning; and the illocutionary force in the second case is a matter

[1] J. O. Urmson, *op. cit.* p. 166.

of the use of the special terms the sentence contains. Illocutionary force can in principle always be made a matter of meaning, but in this case it is not.

It might be thought that this is a trick example because it employs a special or technical term but the same point can be made in terms of other examples. A statement P made in the utterance of a sentence S could entail a statement Q made in the utterance of a sentence T, even though the utterance of S characteristically had one illocutionary force and the utterance of T had another illocutionary force. Suppose a man gives an elaborate statement of his criteria for assessing cars. Suppose further that he gives an elaborate description of his car. Suppose also that the conjunction of criteria and description are sufficient to entail that the car meets the criteria; that is, they are sufficient to entail that, by the speaker's lights, it is a good car. Still, in giving the criteria and the description, the man still has not *said* it is a good car; nor, without making further assumptions about the man's intentions, can it yet be said that in giving criteria and descriptions he had even praised the car. The man is indeed *committed* to the view that it is a good car, for what he says entails that on his criteria it is a good car; but having such a commitment is not at all the same as actually having asserted that it is a good car.

Perhaps the best examples of the distinction between meaning (in the sense which includes truth conditions) and use are provided by English obscenities. Obscenities are synonymous with, i.e., have the same meaning as, their clinical equivalents. Indeed, the point or one of the points of having the clinical equivalent is to have a polite synonym. But of course the use of obscenities is quite different from the use of their polite synonyms. So a person may be quite willing to assert a proposition using the clinical euphemism and yet quite unwilling to assert the same, and hence entailed, proposition using the obscene word. Take any English obscenity O and its polite clinical equivalent C. The proposition, "If Cx then Ox" is analytic, if we are prepared to use the obscene expression at all. The proposition "Cx" entails the proposition "Ox", but asserting that proposition in the terminology of "Cx" is quite different from asserting it in the form "Ox". For asserting "Ox" in public you can go to jail.[1]

---

[1] *People v. Goldberg et al.* unpublished trial court case, Berkeley Superior Court, California, 1965.

An example of a word that has become something of an obscenity is "nigger". "Nigger" is a rude (impolite, obscene) expression for "Negro". It is sometimes said that "nigger" has both descriptive and evaluative meaning, but this is clearly muddled; for if it were true then there ought to be nothing improper about uttering the sentence, "He is not a nigger", as it would merely be denying the negative evaluative force of "nigger", like saying, "He is not a scoundrel". But the utterance of, "He is not a nigger", is just as improper as, "He is a nigger"; the very utterance of that particular word is an indication of hostility, contempt, etc., for Negroes and is, therefore, taboo.

We have by no means exhausted the topic of the *naturalistic fallacy fallacy* and we shall return to quite different sorts of cases, cases involving institutional facts, in chapter 8.

Chapter 7

PROBLEMS OF REFERENCE

I now wish to consider how the theory of reference advanced in chapter 4 applies to two traditional problems in the philosophy of language, Russell's *theory of definite descriptions*, and the meaning of proper names.

7.1 *The theory of descriptions*

Russell's famous theory of definite descriptions has many different aspects, and in the course of Russell's writings appears to go through different phases. I wish to consider only one element of Russell's theory. Russell says that any sentence of the form "the *f* is *g*", (where "the *f*" has a "primary" occurrence) can be exactly translated, or analyzed as a sentence of the form

$$(\exists x)\,(fx\cdot(y)\,(fy \rightarrow y = x)\cdot gx)$$

Henceforth, when I refer to the theory of descriptions it is this thesis which I am discussing.[1]

How shall the theory be construed? As a minimal thesis we could interpret the theory of descriptions as a proposal for the translation of certain expressions into the predicate calculus, a translation whose only merit is technical convenience. We can regard the relation between definite descriptions in ordinary speech and their Russellian translation as analogous to the relation of the "if" in ordinary speech to the material implication sign of the calculus of truth functions. In neither case is the latter expression to be interpreted as an analysis of the former but as merely an analogue retaining certain features and sacrificing others. With the theory of descriptions so construed I have no quarrel. Where no claim is made no rebuttal is in order.

On the other hand we could treat the theory of descriptions as it was originally intended, i.e., as an analysis of actual language. Frege's theory of sense and reference was originally intended as

[1] I shall ignore the occurrence of definite descriptions in intensional contexts.

an analysis of language, a description of how referring expressions work; and, as a matter of historical fact, Russell intended his theory as an alternative and rival account to Frege's. Frege asked the question what is the relation between a referring expression and its referent? And his answer was that the sense of the referring expression provides the "mode of presentation" of the referent. Reference is in virtue of sense. Russell rejects the question. For him there is no relation between definite descriptions and their referents; rather the sentence containing such an expression is a disguised form of a sentence asserting the existence of an object.[1] It is on this basis that I shall now consider the claims of the theory of descriptions.

The theory of descriptions has been vigorously and convincingly attacked by several writers, notably Strawson[2] and Geach.[3] Why then do I think the issue worth resuming? Am I not beating a dead horse? The issue is worth resuming because too much of the controversy in the literature has centered around the assumptions which led Russell to the theory in the first place, and this has led to a concentration on how the notions of negation and falsity operate with regard to assertions *to the exclusion of all other kinds of illocutionary acts*. This concentration on assertions leaves the attackers fighting with the least effective weapons which are to hand and the defenders, scoring in one or two minor skirmishes, thinking they have won. Indeed, some of the disputants erroneously think that the whole controversy can be solved by settling one issue: would we more naturally say of assertions guilty of reference failure, e.g., "The king of France is bald", that they were false, or would we be reluctant to say that they were either true or false? If we would say that they are false, so it is alleged, the theory of descriptions is correct, if not, not. The illusion that the controversy is really about this point engenders an eristic search for trick examples, at the expense of any serious examination of the way the theory of descriptions fails to conform to any coherent general theory of illocutionary acts.

It does not matter much whether we say of the assertion "The king of France is bald" that it is false or pointless or what not,

---

[1] He also thought Frege's account was internally incoherent. Cf. J. Searle, 'Russell's objections to Frege's theory of sense and reference', *Analysis* (1958).

[2] 'On referring', *Mind* (1950).

[3] 'Russell's Theory of Descriptions', *Analysis* (1950).

as long as we understand *how* it goes wrong. The fact that in ordinary speech we might be reluctant to describe it as just false is only a symptom that something is amiss with any theory which, like the theory of descriptions, forces us to treat it as a straightforwardly false statement. *One way* for the assertion of a singular subject–predicate proposition to be at fault is for the predicate expression to be false of the object referred to by the subject expression. *Quite another way* is for there to be no object referred to by the subject expression for the predicate expression to be either true or false of. We can, if we like, regard both as cases of falsehood and distinguish accordingly between "external" and "internal" negation. But to do so, though not wrong, threatens to obscure the profound difference between the two. To put my point here at its strongest: even if we should discover, *contra* Strawson, that most English speakers would characterize the above assertion as false, this would not affect the case against the theory of descriptions at all.

The way to assess the theory is to examine it in terms of the general theory of speech acts outlined in chapters 1–5. So examined, the fundamental objection to it is simply this: it presents the propositional act of definite reference, when performed with definite descriptions (or, according to Russell, even with ordinary proper names), as equivalent to the illocutionary act of asserting a uniquely existential proposition, and there is no coherent way to integrate such a theory into a theory of illocutionary acts. Under no condition is a propositional act identical with the illocutionary act of assertion, for a propositional act can only occur as part of some illocutionary act, never simply by itself. To make an assertion, on the other hand, is to perform a complete illocutionary act. An attempt such as Russell's to assimilate a kind of propositional act to assertions results in breakdowns as soon as we consider the occurrence of such propositional acts in kinds of illocutionary acts other than assertions, as we shall see.

How does it come about that reference is presented as equivalent to a species of assertion? A statement of the form "The f is g" comes out in the Russellian translation as

$$(\exists x)(fx \cdot (y)(fy \to y = x) \cdot gx)$$

Apart from the predicate, in the original we have just a referring expression, which is not a sentence and not enough to perform an illocutionary act. But the translation contains enough apart from the portion containing the original predicate expression for the performance of the act of assertion: it must do so to satisfy Russell's desire to say of anyone asserting a proposition guilty of reference failure that he is asserting a false proposition. There must be a complete assertion made in the utterance of the sentence even if there is no object for the original predicate to be true or false of.

Now it might be said that this is not an objection to Russell: maybe referring is just a kind of asserting and we are begging the question in supposing it not to be. The way to meet this objection is first to show the weaknesses of the argument which might lead us to accept the Russellian analysis and secondly to show the unfortunate consequences of such an acceptance when we attempt to generalize it.

The whole plausibility of the theory of descriptions, once the paradoxes have been removed, derives from the fact that a precondition of any successfully performed reference is the existence of the object referred to (axiom of existence). And consequently the proposition containing that reference cannot be true if the proposition that the object exists is not true. But, as a perfectly general point, it never simply follows from the fact that a type of act can only be performed under certain conditions, that the performance of that act is itself an assertion that those conditions obtain. No one would suppose that my hitting X is an assertion that X exists, though X's existence is as much a condition of my successfully hitting X as it is of my successfully referring to X. Once we see that what appears to offer support to the theory of descriptions, namely that one cannot truly assert something of the form "The f is g" unless there is an object referred to by "the f", offers it in fact no support at all, it remains only to observe the consequences of generalizing the analysis through all kinds of illocutionary acts.

Reference, we saw, can be common to a wide variety of illocutionary acts, not only to assertions, but to questions, commands, promises, etc. And surely a consistent adherence to the theory of descriptions would lead us to adopt the same analysis of the same referring expressions in all of these. But are we really going to say that anyone who asks, "Is the king of France bald?" or who orders, "Take this to the king of France!" is in fact making a false *assertion*, on the grounds that there is no king of France? Or shall we say, on the other hand, but equally absurdly, that anyone who asks the question, "Is the king of France bald?" is really asking, among other things, whether or not there exists a king of France? What I am trying to show here is that as soon as we try to apply the theory *generally* to all kinds of speech acts, its weakness becomes obvious, and obvious in ways which the preoccupation with *assertions* or statements conceals from us.

Let us scrutinize the application of the Russellian analysis to all kinds of illocutionary acts more closely. As soon as we attempt to analyze questions, commands, etc., on the theory we are faced with a dilemma: either we must construe every illocutionary act which involves a definite description as really two speech acts, an assertion of an existential proposition *plus* some question or command about the object asserted to exist, or we must construe the type of speech act which the original sentence was used to perform as covering the whole of the translation, including the existential sentence. For example, either we must construe "Is the king of France bald?" as "There is one and only one thing which is a king of France. Is that thing bald?" or "Is there one and only one thing which is king of France and is that thing bald?" Symbolically, letting " $\vdash$ " be an illocutionary force indicator for assertions and " ?" be an illocutionary force indicator for questions and letting square brackets indicate the scope of the illocutionary force indicator, we have a choice between:

1. $\vdash[(\exists x)(fx\cdot(y)(fy \to y = x)] \cdot ?[gx)]^1$ and
2. $?[(\exists x)(fx\cdot(y)(fy \to y = x)\cdot gx)]$

But both interpretations involve us in absurdities. Consider a general application of the second alternative. Can we plausibly suppose that every questioner who uses a definite description is questioning the existence of the referent of the definite description? But questions are not the worst sufferers; commands become unconstruable. No one could possibly suppose that "Take this to the king of France!" commands the existence of the king of France. Furthermore, some perfectly sensible locutions become self-contradictory, e.g., the sentence "Suppose the author of *Waverley* had never written *Waverley*", which can in ordinary speech be uttered to express a meaningful supposition, must on

---

[1] No. 1 assumes that quantifiers can sometimes reach across illocutionary force indicators. This seems to be a reasonable assumption since pronouns do it in natural languages: e.g. "A man came. Did you see him?"

this interpretation be translated as "Suppose it had been the case that there were one and only one thing which wrote *Waverley* and that thing did not write *Waverley*", which is not a meaningful supposition but a contradiction. So this interpretation cannot be made to work, and we must, therefore, try the other possible interpretation.

Every illocutionary act in which a definite description is used referringly is to be construed as the assertion of an existential proposition *plus* some other speech act about the object asserted to exist. But this again has absurd consequences. We would regard it as absurd to greet the command, "Take this to the queen of England", with "What you say is true, she does exist". The retort is absurd because the command is not an assertion, nor does it contain an assertion. Again, it is absurd to suppose that someone who asks "Does the queen of England know the king of France?" makes two assertions, one of them true and one false. Of course we would point out to someone who asked such a question that his utterance was defective as a question, that it did not admit of an answer, but this is quite another thing from charging him with having made a false assertion, for he did not make any assertion at all; he asked, or purported to ask, a question. The whole institution of referring is a different sort of institution from asserting or questioning or commanding. Referring is not on the same level with these, for it is a part of a successful illocutionary act, and not itself a kind of illocutionary act. Hence, the absurdity of trying to interpret every illocutionary act involving a definite description as containing an assertion.

These are the only two plausible ways of applying the theory of descriptions to all kinds of illocutionary acts. Neither works. The theory should, therefore, be abandoned.

7.2 *Proper names*

At first sight nothing seems easier to understand in the philosophy of language than our use of proper names: here is the name, there is the object. The name stands for the object.

Although this account is obviously true, it explains nothing. What is meant by "stands for"? And how is the relation indicated by "stands for" ever set up in the first place? Do proper names "stand for" in the same way that definite descriptions "stand for"? These and other questions which I wish to attack in this section can be summed up in the question, "Do proper names have senses?" What this question asks, as a start, is what, if any, similarity is there between the way a definite description picks out its referent and the way a proper name picks out its referent. Is a proper name really a shorthand description? We shall see that the two opposing answers given to this question arise from the tension between, on the one hand, the almost exclusive use of proper names to perform the speech act of reference, and, on the other hand, the means and preconditions for performing this speech act which we discussed in chapter 4—especially the condition expressed in the principle of identification.

The first answer goes something like this: proper names do not have senses, they are meaningless marks; they have denotation but not connotation (Mill).[1] The argument for this view is that whereas a definite description refers to an object only in virtue of the fact that it describes some *aspect* of that object, a proper name does not *describe* the object at all. To know that a definite description fits an object is to know a fact about that object, but to know its name is not so far to know any facts about it. This difference between proper names and definite descriptions is further illustrated by the fact that we can often turn a definite description (a referring expression) into an ordinary predicative expression by simply substituting an indefinite article for the definite, e.g., "a man" for "the man". No such shift is in general possible with proper names. When we do put the indefinite article in front of a proper name it is either a shorthand way of expressing well-known characteristics of the bearer of the name (e.g., "He is a Napoleon" means "He is like Napoleon in many respects"), or it is a shorthand form of a formal-mode expression about the name itself (e.g., "He is a Robert" means "He is named Robert"). In short we use a proper name to refer and not to describe; a proper name predicates nothing and consequently does not have a sense.

Our robust common sense leads us to think that this answer must be right, but though it has enormous plausibility, we shall see that it cannot be right, at least not as it stands, for too many facts militate against it. First, let us look at some of the metaphysical traps that an uncritical acceptance of such a view is likely

[1] J. S. Mill, *A System of Logic* (London and Colchester, 1949), book 1, chapter 2, para. 5.

to lead us into. The proper name, we are inclined to say, is not connected with any *aspects* of the object as descriptions are, it is tied to the object itself. Descriptions stand for aspects or properties of an object, proper names for the real thing. This is the first step on the road that leads to substance, for it fastens on to what is supposed to be a basic metaphysical distinction between objects and properties or aspects of objects, and it derives this distinction from an alleged difference between proper names and definite descriptions. Such a muddle is to be found in the *Tractatus* "The name means the object. The object is its meaning" (3.203).[1] But notice to what interesting paradoxes this leads to immediately: the meaning of words, it seems, cannot depend on any contingent facts in the world, for we can still describe the world even if the facts alter. Yet the existence of ordinary objects—people, cities, etc.—is contingent, and hence the existence of any meaning for their names is contingent. So their names are not the real names at all! There must exist a class of objects whose existence is not a contingent fact, and it is their names which are the real names.[2] And what does this mean? Here we see another good illustration of the original sin of all metaphysics, the attempt to read real or alleged features of language into the world.

The usual rejoinder to the thesis that there is a basic metaphysical distinction between objects and properties is that objects are just collections of properties.[3] The first thesis is derived from the distinction between referring and predicating, the second thesis is derived from the tautology that everything that can be said about an object can be said in descriptions of that object. But both theses are equally nonsensical. It is nonsense to suppose that an object is a combination of its propertyless self and its properties, and it is nonsense to suppose that an object is a heap or collection of properties. Again, both views have a common origin in the metaphysical mistake of deriving ontological conclusions from linguistic theses.

There are three objections to the view that proper names do not have senses:

1. We use proper names in existential propositions, e.g., "there

[1] Mill's: proper names have no meaning, might appear to be inconsistent with Wittgenstein's: objects are their meanings. But they are not inconsistent. (Ambiguity of "mean" and "bedeuten".) Both say, proper names have referents but not senses. [2] Cf. also Plato, *Theaetetus*.
[3] E.g., Russell, *An Inquiry into Meaning and Truth* (London, 1940), p. 97.

is such a place as Africa", "Cerberus does not exist". Here proper names cannot be said to refer, for no such subject of an existential statement can refer. If it did, the precondition of its having a truth value would guarantee its truth, if it were in the affirmative, and its falsity, if it were in the negative. (This is just another way of saying that "exists" is not a predicate.) Every existential statement states that a certain predicate is instantiated. (As Frege put it, existence is a second order concept.)[1] An existential statement does not refer to an object and state that it exists, rather it expresses a concept and states that that concept is instantiated. Thus, if a proper name occurs in an existential statement it must have some conceptual or descriptive content. Attempts such as Russell's[2] to evade this point have taken the form of saying that such expressions are not *really* proper names, a desperate maneuver which shows that something must be wrong with the assumptions which drive one to it.

2. Sentences containing proper names can be used to make identity statements which convey factual and not merely linguistic information. Thus the sentence, "Everest is Chomolungma" can be used to make an assertion which has geographical and not merely lexicographical import. Yet if proper names were without senses, then the assertion could convey no more information than does an assertion made with the sentence "Everest is Everest". Thus it seems that proper names must have descriptive content, they must have a sense. This is substantially Frege's argument that proper names have senses.[3]

3. The principle of identification requires that an utterance of a proper name must convey a description just as the utterance of a definite description must if the reference is to be consummated. And from this it seems to follow that a proper name is a kind of shorthand description.

All three objections point to the same conclusion, namely, that proper names are shorthand definite descriptions.

---

[1] *Grundgesetze der Arithmetik* (Jena, 1893), vol. 1, section 21.
[2] 'The Philosophy of Logical Atomism', R. Marsh (ed.), *Logic and Knowledge* (London, 1956), pp. 200 ff.
[3] Though, with a characteristic perversity, he did not see that this account of identity statements provides an explanation of the use of proper names in existential statements. He thought it was nonsense to use proper names in existential statements. 'Über die Grundlagen der Geometrie II', *Jahresbericht der Deutschen Mathematiker-Vereinigung* (1903), p. 373.

But it seems that this conclusion cannot be right, for, aside from its grotesque unplausibility, it is inconsistent with too many obvious truths. First, if it were the case that a proper name is a shorthand description, then descriptions should be available as definitional equivalents for proper names; but we do not, in general, have definitions of proper names. In so called dictionaries of proper names, one finds descriptions of the bearers of the names, but in most cases these descriptions are not definitional equivalents for the names, since they are only contingently true of the bearers.

No only do we not have definitional equivalents, but it is not clear how we could go about getting them to substitute in all cases for proper names. If we try to present a complete description of the object as the sense of the name, odd consequences would ensue, e.g., any true statement about the object using the name as subject would be analytic, any false one self-contradictory, the meaning of the name (and perhaps the identity of the object) would change every time there was any change at all in the object, the name would have different meanings for different people, etc. So it seems that the view that proper names are descriptions cannot be true either.

Here we have a beautiful example of a philosophic problem: on the one hand common sense drives us to the conclusion that a proper name is not a species of description, that it is *sui generis*, but against this a series of theoretical considerations drive us to the conclusion that it must be a shorthand definite description. But against this too we can adduce serious arguments. This antinomy admits of a solution toward which I shall now argue.

We might rephrase our original question, "Do proper names have senses?" as "Do referring uses of proper names entail any descriptive predicates?" or simply "Are any propositions where the subject is a proper name and the predicate a descriptive expression analytic?"[1] But this question has a weaker and a stronger

---

[1] Of course, in one sense of "analytic", no such subject–predicate proposition can be analytic, since it is in general a contingent fact that the subject expression has a referent at all and hence contingent that the proposition has a truth-value. To meet this objection we can either redefine "analytic" as: "p is analytic $= df$. if p has a truth-value, it is true by definition" or we can rephrase the original question as, "Is any proposition of the form "if anything is S it is P" analytic, where "S" is replaced by a proper name and "P" by a descriptive predicate?"

form: (*a*) the weaker: "Are any such statements at all analytic?" and (*b*) the stronger: "Are any statements where the subject is a proper name and the predicate an identifying description analytic?"

Consider the first question. It is characteristic of a proper name that it is used to refer to the *same* object on *different* occasions. The use of the same name at different times in the history of the object presupposes that the object is the same; a necessary condition of identity of reference is identity of the object referred to. But to presuppose that the object is the same in turn presupposes a criterion of identity: that is, it presupposes an ability on the part of the speaker to answer the question, "In virtue of what is the object at time *t*.1, referred by name *N*, identical with the object at time *t*.2, referred to by the same name?" or, put more simply, "The object at time *t*.1 is the same *what* as the object at time *t*.2?" and the gap indicated by "what" is to be filled by a descriptive general term; it is the same mountain, the same person, the same river, the general term providing in each case a temporal criterion of identity. This gives us an affirmative answer to the weaker question. Some general term is analytically tied to any proper name: Everest is a mountain, the Mississippi is a river, de Gaulle is a person. Anything which was not a mountain could not be Everest, etc., for to secure continuity of reference we need a criterion of identity, and the general term associated with the name provides the criterion. Even for those people who would want to assert that de Gaulle could turn into a tree or horse and still be de Gaulle, there must be some identity criterion. De Gaulle could not turn into anything whatever, e.g., a prime number, and still remain de Gaulle, and to say this is to say that some term or range of terms is analytically tied to the name "de Gaulle".

To forestall an objection: one temptation is to say that if we continue to call an object "Everest", the property of being called "Everest" is sufficient to guarantee that it is the same. But the point of the above analysis is that we are only justified in calling it "Everest" if we can give a reason for supposing it to be identical with what we used to call "Everest" and to give as the reason that it is called "Everest" would be circular. In this sense at least, proper names do have 'connotations'.

But the answer "yes" to the weaker question does not entail the same answer to the stronger one, and it is the stronger form which is crucial for deciding whether or not a proper name has a sense, as Frege and I use the word. For according to Frege the sense of a proper name contains the "mode of presentation" which identifies the referent, and of course a single descriptive predicate does not provide us with a mode of presentation; it does not provide an identifying description. That Socrates is a man may be analytically true, but the predicate "man" is not an identifying description of Socrates.

So let us consider the stronger formulation of our question in the light of the principle of identification. According to this principle, anyone who uses a proper name must be prepared to substitute an identifying description (remembering that identifying descriptions include ostensive presentations) of the object referred to by a proper name. If he were unable to do this, we should say that he did not know whom or what he was talking about, and it is this consideration which inclines us, and which among other things inclined Frege, to say that a proper name must have a sense, and that the identifying description constitutes that sense. Think what it is to learn a proper name. Suppose you say to me: "Consider Thaklakes, tell me what you think of Thaklakes." If I have never heard that name before I can only reply, "Who is he?" or "What is it?" And does not your next move—which according to the principle of identification consists in giving me an ostensive presentation or a set of descriptions—does this not give me the sense of the name, just as you might give me the sense of a general term? Is this not a definition of the name?

We have discussed several objections to this view already; a further one is that the description one man is prepared to substitute for the name may not be the same as the one someone else is prepared to substitute. Are we to say that what is definitionally true for one is only contingent for another? Notice what maneuvers Frege is forced to here:

> "Suppose further that Herbert Garner knows that Dr Gustav Lauben was born on 13 September 1875, in N. H. and this is not true of anyone else; against this suppose that he does not know where Dr Lauben now lives or indeed anything about him. On the other hand, suppose Leo Peter does not know that Dr Lauben was born on 13 September 1875, in N. H. Then as far as the proper name "Dr Gustav Lauben" is concerned, Herbert Garner and Leo Peter do not speak the

same language, since, although they do in fact refer to the same man with this name, they do not know that they do so."[1]

Thus according to Frege, unless our descriptive backing for the name is the same, we are not even speaking the same language. But, against this, notice that we seldom consider a proper name as part of *one* language as opposed to another at all.

Furthermore, I might discover that my identifying description was not true of the object in question and still not abandon his name. I may learn the use of "Aristotle" by being told that it is the name of the Greek philosopher born in Stagira, but if later scholars assure me that Aristotle was not born in Stagira at all but in Thebes, I will not accuse them of self-contradiction. But let us scrutinize this more closely: scholars might discover that a *particular* belief commonly held about Aristotle was false. But does it make sense to suppose that everything anyone has ever believed to be true of Aristotle was in fact not true of the real Aristotle? Clearly not, and this will provide us with the germ of an answer to our question.

Suppose we ask the users of the name "Aristotle" to state what they regard as certain essential and established facts about him. Their answers would constitute a set of identifying descriptions, and I wish to argue that though no single one of them is analytically true of Aristotle, their disjunction is. Put it this way: suppose we have independent means of identifying an object, what then are the conditions under which I could say of the object, "This is Aristotle?" I wish to claim that the conditions, the descriptive power of the statement, is that a sufficient but so far unspecified number of these statements (or descriptions) are true of the object. In short, if none of the identifying descriptions believed to be true of some object by the users of the name of that object proved to be true of some independently located object, then that object could not be identical with the bearer of the name. It is a necessary condition for an object to be Aristotle that it satisfy at least some of these descriptions. This is another way of saying that the disjunction of these descriptions is analytically tied to the name "Aristotle"—which is a quasi-affirmative answer to the question, "Do proper names have senses?" in its stronger formulation.

[1] 'The Thought: a logical inquiry', trans. by A. and M. Quinton, *Mind* (1956), p. 297.

My answer, then, to the question, "Do proper names have senses?"—if this asks whether or not proper names are used to describe or specify characteristics of objects—is "No". But if it asks whether or not proper names are logically connected with characteristics of the object to which they refer, the answer is "Yes, in a loose sort of way".

Some philosophers suppose that it is an objection to this sort of account that the same word is sometimes used as a name for more than one object. But this is a totally irrelevant fact and not an objection to my account at all. That different objects are named "John Smith" is no more relevant to the question "Do proper names have senses?" than the fact that both riversides and finance houses are called "banks" is relevant to the question, "Do general terms have senses?" Both "bank" and "John Smith" suffer from kinds of homonymy, but one does not prove a word meaningless by pointing out that it has several meanings. I should have considered this point too obvious to need stating, were it not for the fact that almost every philosopher to whom I have presented this account makes this objection.

What I have said is a sort of compromise between Mill and Frege. Mill was right in thinking that proper names do not entail any particular description, that they do not have definitions, but Frege was correct in assuming that any singular term must have a mode of presentation and hence, in a way, a sense. His mistake was in taking the identifying description which we can substitute for the name as a definition.

I should point out, parenthetically, that of course the description, "The man called X" will not do, or at any rate will not do by itself, as a satisfaction of the principle of identification. For if you ask me, "Whom do you mean by X?" and I answer, "The man called X", even if it were true that there is only one man who is called X, I am simply saying that he is the man whom other people refer to by the name "X". But if they refer to him by the name "X" then they must also be prepared to substitute an identifying description for "X" and if they in their turn substitute "the man called X", the question is only carried a stage further and cannot go on indefinitely without circularity or infinite regress. My reference to an individual may be parasitic on someone else's but this parasitism cannot be carried on indefinitely if there is to be any reference at all.

For this reason it is no answer at all to the question of what if anything is the sense of a proper name "*X*" to say its sense or part of its sense is "called *X*". One might as well say that part of the meaning of "horse" is "called a horse". It is really quite amazing how often this mistake is made.[1]

My analysis of proper names enables us to account for all the apparently inconsistent views at the beginning of this section. How is it possible that a proper name can occur in an existential statement? A statement such as "Aristotle never existed" states that a sufficient, but so far unspecified, number of the descriptive backings of "Aristotle" are false. Which one of these is asserted to be false is not yet clear, for the descriptive backing of "Aristotle" is not yet precise. Suppose that of the propositions believed to be true of Aristotle half were true of one man and half of another, would we say that Aristotle never existed? The question is not decided for us in advance.

Similarly it is easy to explain identity statements using proper names. "Everest is Chomolungma" states that the descriptive backing of both names is true of the same object. If the descriptive backing of the two names, for the person making the assertion, is the same, or if one contains the other, the statement is analytic, if not, synthetic. Frege's instinct was sound in inferring from the fact that we do make factually informative identity statements using proper names that they must have a sense, but he was wrong in supposing that this sense is as straightforward as in a definite description. His famous "Morning Star–Evening Star" example led him astray here, for though the sense of these names is fairly straightforward, these expressions are not paradigm proper names, but are on the boundary line between definite descriptions and proper names.

Furthermore, we now see how an utterance of a proper name satisfies the principle of identification: if both the speaker and the hearer associate some identifying description with the name, then the utterance of the name is sufficient to satisfy the principle of identification, for both the speaker and the hearer are able to substitute an identifying description. The utterance of the name communicates a proposition to the hearer. It is not necessary that both should supply the same identifying description, provided only that their descriptions are in fact true of the same object.

[1] E.g., A. Church, *Introduction to Mathematical Logic* (Princeton, 1956), p. 5.

We have seen that insofar as proper names can be said to have a sense, it is an imprecise one. We must now explore the reasons for this imprecision. Is the imprecision as to what characteristics exactly constitute the necessary and sufficient conditions for applying a proper name a mere accident, a product of linguistic slovenliness? Or does it derive from the functions which proper names perform for us? To ask for the criteria for applying the name "Aristotle" is to ask in the formal mode what Aristotle is; it is to ask for a set of identity criteria for the object Aristotle. "What is Aristotle?" and "What are the criteria for applying the name "Aristotle"?" ask the same question, the former in the material mode, and the latter in the formal mode of speech. So if, prior to using the name, we came to an agreement on the precise characteristics which constituted the identity of Aristotle, our rules for using the name would be precise. But this precision would be achieved only at the cost of entailing some *specific* descriptions by any use of the name. Indeed, the name itself would become logically equivalent to this set of descriptions. But if this were the case we would be in the position of being able to refer to an object solely by, in effect, describing it. Whereas in fact this is just what the institution of proper names enables us to avoid and what distinguishes proper names from definite descriptions. If the criteria for proper names were in all cases quite rigid and specific, then a proper name would be nothing more than a shorthand for these criteria, it would function exactly like an elaborate definite description. But the uniqueness and immense pragmatic convenience of proper names in our language lies precisely in the fact that they enable us to refer publicly to objects without being forced to raise issues and come to an agreement as to which descriptive characteristics exactly constitute the identity of the object. They function not as descriptions, but as pegs on which to hang descriptions. Thus the looseness of the criteria for proper names is a necessary condition for isolating the referring function from the describing function of language.

To put the same point differently, suppose we ask, "Why do we have proper names at all?" Obviously, to refer to individuals. "Yes, but descriptions could do that for us." But only at the cost of specifying identity conditions every time reference is made: suppose we agree to drop "Aristotle" and use, say, "the teacher of Alexander", then it is an analytic truth that the man referred to is

Alexander's teacher—but it is a contingent fact that Aristotle ever went into pedagogy. (Though it is, as I have said, a necessary truth that Aristotle has the logical sum [inclusive disjunction] of the properties commonly attributed to him.)[1]

It should not be thought that the only sort of looseness of identity criteria for individuals is that which I have described as peculiar to proper names. Identity problems of quite different sorts may arise, for instance, from referring uses of definite descriptions. "This is the man who taught Alexander" may be said to entail, e.g., that this object is spatio-temporally continuous with the man teaching Alexander at another point in space-time; but someone might also argue that this man's spatio-temporal continuity is a contingent characteristic and not an identity criterion. And the logical nature of the connection of such characteristics with the man's identity may again be loose and undecided in advance of dispute. But this is quite another dimension of looseness from that which I cited as the looseness of the criteria for applying proper names, and does not affect the distinction in function between definite descriptions and proper names, viz., that definite descriptions refer only in virtue of the fact that the criteria are not loose in the original sense, for they refer by providing an explicit description of the object. But proper names refer without providing such a description.

We might clarify some of the points made in this chapter by comparing paradigm proper names with degenerate proper names like "the Bank of England". For these limiting cases of proper names, it seems the sense is given as straightforwardly as in a definite description; the presuppositions, as it were, rise to the surface. And a proper name may acquire a rigid use without having the verbal form of a description: God is just, omnipotent, omniscient, etc., *by definition* for believers. To us, "Homer" just means "the author of the *Iliad* and the *Odyssey*". The form may often mislead us: the Holy Roman Empire was neither holy nor Roman, etc., but it was, nonetheless, the Holy Roman Empire. Again, it may be conventional to name only girls "Martha", but if I name my son "Martha", I may mislead, but I do not lie. And of course not all paradigm proper names are alike with respect to the nature of their 'descriptive content'. There will, e.g., be a difference

---

[1] Ignoring contradictory properties, $pv \sim p$ would render the logical sum trivially true.

between the names of living people, where the capacity of the user of the name to recognize the person may be an important 'identifying description', and the names of historical figures. But the essential fact to keep in mind when dealing with these problems is that we have the institution of proper names to perform the speech act of identifying reference. The existence of these expressions derives from our need to separate the referring from the predicating functions of language. But we never get referring completely isolated from predication for to do so would be to violate the principle of identification, without conformity to which we cannot refer at all.

Chapter 8

DERIVING "OUGHT" FROM "IS"

One of the oldest of metaphysical distinctions is that between fact and value. Underlying the belief in this distinction is the perception that values somehow derive from persons and cannot lie in the world, at least not in the world of stones, rivers, trees, and brute facts. For if they did, they would cease to be values and would become simply another part of that world. One trouble with the distinction in the history of philosophy is that there have been many different ways of characterizing it, and they are not all equivalent. Hume is commonly supposed to have been alluding to it in a famous passage in the *Treatise* where he speaks of the vicissitudes of moving from "is" to "ought".[1] Moore saw the distinction in terms of the difference between "natural" properties like yellow, and what he called "non-natural" properties, like goodness.[2] Ironically, Moore's successors, reversing the usual order of metaphysical progression, have read this metaphysical distinction back into language as a thesis about entailment relations in language. So construed it is a thesis that no set of descriptive statements can entail an evaluative statement. I say "ironically" because language, of all places, is riddled with counter-instances to the view that no evaluations can follow from descriptions. As we saw in chapter 6, to call an argument valid is already to evaluate it and yet the statement that it is valid follows from certain 'descriptive' statements about it. The very notions of what it is to be a valid argument, a cogent argument, a good piece of reasoning are evaluative in the relevant sense because, e.g., they involve the notions of what one is *justified* or *right* in concluding, given certain premises. The irony, in short, lies in the fact that the very terminology in which the thesis is expressed—the terminology of entailment, meaning, and validity—presupposes the falsity of the thesis. For example, the statement that *p* entails *q* entails, among other things, that

[1] D. Hume, *A Treatise of Human Nature* (L. A. Selby-Bigge, ed.), (Oxford, 1888), p. 469. It is not so clear that this interpretation of Hume is right. Cf. A. C. MacIntyre, 'Hume on "is" and "ought"', *The Philosophical Review*, vol. 67 (1959).

[2] G. E. Moore, *Principia Ethica* (Cambridge, 1903).

anyone who asserts *p* is *committed* to the truth of *q*, and that if *p* is known to be true then one is *justified* in concluding that *q*. And the notions of commitment and justification in such cases are no more and no less 'evaluative' than they are when we speak of being committed to doing something or being justified in declaring war.

In this chapter I want to probe deeper into the alleged impossibility of deriving an evaluative statement from a set of descriptive statements. Using the conclusions of the analysis of illocutionary acts in chapter 3, I shall attempt to demonstrate another counter-example to this thesis.[1]

The thesis that "ought" cannot be derived from "is" is generally regarded as simply another way of stating, or a special case of, the view that descriptive statements cannot entail evaluative statements. A counter-example to this thesis must proceed by taking a statement or statements which a proponent of the thesis would regard as purely factual or descriptive (they need not actually contain the word "is") and show how they are logically related to a statement which a proponent of the thesis would regard as evaluative (in the present instance, it will contain an "ought").[2]

Let us remind ourselves at the outset that "ought" is a humble English modal auxiliary, "is" an English copula; and the question whether "ought" can be derived from "is" is as humble as the words themselves. One of the obstacles to seeing this matter clearly is what Austin called the "*ivresse des grands profondeurs*". If one is convinced in advance that Great Issues hinge on the question of whether "ought" can be derived from "is", then one may have real difficulty getting a clear picture of the logical and linguistic issues involved. In particular we must avoid, at least initially, lapsing into talk about ethics or morals. We are concerned with "ought", not "morally ought". If one accepts such a distinction, one could say that I am concerned with a thesis in the philosophy of language, not a thesis in moral philosophy. I think that the question whether "ought" can be derived from "is" does indeed

---

[1] In its modern version. I shall not be concerned to present counter-examples to the views of Hume, Moore, or to the metaphysical distinction between fact and value.

[2] If this enterprise succeeds, we shall again have bridged the gap between "evaluative" and "descriptive" and consequently have demonstrated another weakness in this very terminology. At present, however, my strategy is to play along with the terminology, pretending that the notions of evaluative and descriptive are fairly clear. Later in this chapter I shall state in what respects I think they embody a muddle, in addition to the fallacy discussed in chapter 6.

have a bearing on moral philosophy but I shall discuss that after I present my counter-example. If one reads the standard authors on the subject of " ought " and " is " one is impressed by the extent to which they are looking over their shoulders at moral and even political questions at the expense of a concern for modal auxiliaries and illocutionary forces.

What follows is substantially the same as a proof I published earlier.[1] Published criticisms of that earlier work make it clear to me that it is worth stating again; to clear up misunderstandings, to meet objections, and to integrate its conclusions within the general account of speech acts.

8.1 *How to do it*

Consider the following series of statements:

1. Jones uttered the words " I hereby promise to pay you, Smith, five dollars ".

2. Jones promised to pay Smith five dollars.

3. Jones placed himself under (undertook) an obligation to pay Smith five dollars.

4. Jones is under an obligation to pay Smith five dollars.

5. Jones ought to pay Smith five dollars.

I shall argue concerning this list that the relation between any statement and its successor, while not in every case one of entailment, is nonetheless not just an accidental or completely contingent relation; and the additional statements and certain other adjustments necessary to make the relationship one of entailment do not need to involve any evaluative statements, moral principles, or anything of the sort.

Let us begin. How is 1 related to 2? In certain circumstances, uttering the words in quotation marks in 1 is the act of making a promise. And it is a part of or a consequence of the meaning of the words in 1 that in those circumstances uttering them is promising. " I hereby promise " is a paradigm device in English for performing the act identified in 2, promising.

Let us state this empirical fact about English usage in the form of an extra premise:

1 *a*. Under certain conditions *C* anyone who utters the words

---

[1] J. R. Searle, 'How to derive " ought " from " is "', *The Philosophical Review* (January 1964).

(sentence) "I hereby promise to pay you, Smith, five dollars" promises to pay Smith five dollars.

What sorts of things are involved under the rubric "conditions *C*"? The conditions will be those which we specified in chapter 3, the necessary and sufficient conditions for the utterance of the words (sentence) to constitute the successful and non-defective performance of the act of promising. This includes the input and output conditions, the various intentions and beliefs of the speaker, and so on (see section 3.1). As I pointed out in chapter 3, the boundaries of the concept of a promise are, like the boundaries of most concepts in a natural language, a bit loose. But one thing is clear; however loose the boundaries may be, and however difficult it may be to decide marginal cases, the conditions under which a man who utters "I hereby promise" can correctly be said to have made a promise are in a perfectly ordinary sense empirical conditions.

So let us add as an extra premise the empirical assumption that these conditions obtain.

1*b*. Conditions *C* obtain.

From 1, 1*a*, and 1*b* we derive 2. The argument is of the form: If *C* then (if *U* then *P*): *C* for conditions, *U* for utterance, *P* for promise. Adding the premises *U* and *C* to this hypothetical we derive 2. And as far as I can see, no evaluative premises are lurking in the logical woodpile. More needs to be said about the relation of 1 to 2, but I shall reserve that for later.

What is the relation between 2 and 3? It follows from our analysis of promising in chapter 3 that promising is, by definition, an act of placing oneself under an obligation. No analysis of the concept of promising will be complete which does not include the feature of the promisor placing himself under or undertaking or accepting or recognizing an obligation to the promisee to perform some future course of action, normally for the benefit of the promisee. One may be tempted to think that promising can be analyzed in terms of creating expectations in one's hearers, or some such, but a little reflection will show that the crucial distinction between statements of intention on the one hand and promises on the other lies in the nature and degree of commitment or obligation undertaken in promising. Therefore, I think 2 entails 3 straight off, but I can have no objection if anyone wishes to add— for the purpose of formal neatness—the tautological (analytic) premise:

2 *a*. All promises are acts of placing oneself under (undertaking) an obligation to do the thing promised.

This derivation is of the *modus ponens* form: if *P* then *PUO*: *P* for promise, *PUO* for place under obligation, adding the premise *P* to this hypothetical we derive 3.[1]

How is 3 related to 4? If one has placed oneself under an obligation, then at the time of the obligating performance, one is under an obligation. That, I take it, also is a tautology or analytic truth, i.e., one cannot have succeeded in placing oneself under an obligation if there is no point at which one was under an obligation. Of course it is possible for all sorts of things to happen *subsequently* which will release one from obligations one has undertaken, but that fact is irrelevant to the tautology that when one places oneself under an obligation one is at that point under an obligation. In order to get a straightforward entailment between 3 and 4 we need only construe 4 in such a way as to exclude any time gap between the point of the completion of the act in which the obligation is undertaken, 3, and the point at which it is claimed the agent is under an obligation, 4. So construed, 3 entails 4 straight off. Formalists may wish to preface each of 1–5 with the phrase "at time *t*", and as in the move from 3 to 4, add the tautological premise:

3 *a*. All those who place themselves under an obligation are (at the time when they so place themselves) under an obligation.

So construed, the move from 3 to 4 is of the same form as the move from 2 to 3. If (at *t*) *PUO* then (at *t*) *UO*: *t* for a particular time, *PUO* for place under obligation, *UO* for under obligation. Adding (at *t*) *PUO* to this hypothetical we derive (at *t*) *UO*.

I am treating the tense of the copula in 4 as tying it rigidly to the time of the act of promising. But, to repeat, another way to make the same point is to preface each of 1–5 with the phrase "at time *t*". In the earlier version of this proof[2] I treated the "is" of 4 as a genuine present and allowed for a time gap between the completion of the act of promising and the "is" of "Jones is under an obligation". I then added a *ceteris paribus* clause to allow for the fact that in the intervening period various things might occur to relieve Jones from the obligation he undertook in promising, e.g., Smith might release him from the obligation, or he might

---

[1] At this point we have already derived an 'evaluative', statement from 'descriptive' statements since "obligation" is an 'evaluative' word.

[2] J. R. Searle, *op. cit.*, pp. 46 ff.

discharge the obligation by paying the money. A similar *ceteris paribus* clause between 4 and 5 dealt with the possibility of conflicting obligations, a possible evil character, or evil consequences of, the promised act, etc. I think that formulation was more true to life in that it explicitly took into consideration the defeasible character of statements like 4 and 5. But the defeasibility has to do with the fact that considerations outside the act of promising bear on what obligations one has or what one ought to do. These considerations do not bear on the logical relations I am here trying to spell out and so are irrelevant to our present concern.

Furthermore, in the present climate of philosophical opinion, leaving the *ceteris paribus* considerations in the derivation proved to be a standing invitation to various kinds of irrelevant objections. One set of my critics even claimed that the belief in the impossibility of deriving evaluative from descriptive statements was based on the need for a *ceteris paribus* clause in the derivations. So, to avoid the introduction of such irrelevancies, in this step and the next, I note in passing but leave out of the proof any explicit consideration of how extraneous factors release, discharge, or override the obligation undertaken when one makes a promise. The essential point for the move from 3 to 4 is the tautology that when you place yourself under an obligation you are then and there under an obligation, even though you may be able to get out of it later, may have conflicting and overriding obligations at the same time, etc.[1]

What is the relationship between 4 and 5? Analogous to the tautology which explicates the relation between 3 and 4 there is here the tautology that if one is under an obligation to do something, then, as regards that obligation, one ought to do what one is under an obligation to do. Of course, to repeat, there may be all sorts of other reasons for saying that one ought not to do an act one is under an obligation to do; e.g., one may have a conflicting obligation not to do the act, or the act may be of such an evil

---

[1] It is perhaps important to emphasize that the fact that an obligation might be outweighed by another obligation or the fact that an obligation might be discharged or excused does not even qualify the obligation, let alone deny its existence. There has to be an obligation in the first place to be countervailed or excused. I may be in a conflict as to which of two conflicting obligations I ought to carry out, which of the two I should perform and which I should breach. I may be justified in not doing what I ought to do as regards a particular obligation. My breach may even be excused, sanctioned, or even encouraged. To all this the fact that I ought to do what I have undertaken an obligation to do is logically anterior.

character or have such evil consequences that one's obligation to do the act is overriden by these considerations, and one ought not, all things considered, to do the act. One can, after all, undertake an obligation to do all sorts of frightful things which one ought not to do. So we need to eliminate these possibilities by making more precise the sense of 5 in which it follows from 4. We need to distinguish

5'. As regards his obligation to pay Smith five dollars, Jones ought to pay Smith five dollars
and

5″. All things considered, Jones ought to pay Smith five dollars. Now clearly if we interpret 5 as 5″ we cannot derive it from 4 without additional premises. But equally clearly if we interpret it as equivalent to 5', which is perhaps the more plausible interpretation given its occurence in the discourse, we can derive it from 4. And regardless of whether we wish to interpret 5 as 5', we can simply derive 5' from 4, which is quite sufficient for our present purposes. Here, as in the two previous steps, we can add, for purposes of formal neatness, the tautological premise:

4a. If one is under an obligation to do something, then as regards that obligation one ought to do what one is under an obligation to do.

This argument is of the form: If *UO* then (as regards *UO*) *O*. *UO* for under obligation, *O* for ought. Adding the premise *UO* we derive (as regards *UO*) *O*.

We have thus derived (in as strict a sense of "derive" as natural language will admit of) an "ought" from an "is". And the extra premises which were needed to make the derivation work were in no case moral or evaluative in nature. They consisted of empirical assumptions, tautologies, and descriptions of word usage. It must be pointed out also that even with 5 interpreted as 5' the "ought" is in Kant's sense a "categorical" not a "hypothetical" ought. 5' does not say that Jones ought to pay up *if he wants such and such.* It says he ought, as regards his obligation, to pay up. Note also that the steps of the derivation are carried on in the third person. We are not concluding "I ought" from "I said "I promise"", but "he ought" from "he said "I promise"".

The proof unfolds the connection between the utterance of certain words and the speech act of promising and then in turn unfolds promising into obligation and moves from obligation to "ought". The step from 1 to 2 is radically different from the others and requires special comment. In 1 we construe "I hereby promise..." as an English phrase having a certain meaning. It is a consequence of that meaning that the utterance of that phrase under certain conditions is the act of promising. Thus, by presenting the quoted expressions in 1 and by describing their use in 1 *a* we have as it were already invoked the institution of promising. We might have started with an even more ground-floor premise than 1 by saying:

1 *b*. Jones uttered the phonetic sequence: /ai⁺ hɪrbai⁺ pramis⁺ təpei⁺ yu⁺ smiθ⁺ faiv⁺ dalərz/

We would then have needed extra empirical premises stating that this phonetic sequence was correlated in certain ways with certain meaningful units relative to certain dialects.

The moves from 2 and 5′ are relatively easy because formally each is mediated by a tautology. We rely on definitional connections between "promise", "obligate", and "ought", and the only problems which arise are that obligations can be overridden or removed in a variety of ways and we need to take account of that fact. We solve our difficulty by specifying that the existence of the obligation is at the time of the undertaking of the obligation, and the "ought" is relative to the existence of the obligation.

8.2 *The nature of the issues involved*

Even supposing what I have said so far is true, still, readers brought up on contemporary philosophy will feel a certain uneasiness. They will feel that there must be some trick involved somewhere. We might state their uneasiness thus: How can my granting a mere fact about a man, such as the fact that he uttered certain words or that he made a promise, commit *me* to the view that *he* ought to do something? I now want briefly to discuss what broader philosophic significance my attempted derivation may have, in such a way as to give us the outlines of an answer to this question.

I shall begin by discussing the grounds for supposing that it cannot be answered at all.

The inclination to accept a rigid distinction between "is" and "ought", and similarly between descriptive and evaluative, rests on a certain picture of the way words relate to the world. It is a very attractive picture, so attractive (to me at least) that it is not entirely clear to what extent the mere presentation of counter-examples of the sort I presented here and in chapter 6 can challenge it. What is needed is an explanation of how and why this classical empiricist picture fails to deal with such counter-examples. Briefly, the picture is constructed something like this: first we present examples of so-called descriptive statements ("My car goes eighty miles an hour", "Jones is six feet tall", "Smith has brown hair"), and we contrast them with so-called evaluative statements ("my car is a good car", "Jones ought to pay Smith five dollars", "Smith is a nasty man"). Anyone can see that they are different. We articulate the difference by pointing out that for the descriptive statements the question of truth or falsity is objectively decidable, because to know the meaning of the descriptive expressions is to know under what objectively ascertainable conditions the statements which contain them are true or false. But in the case of evaluative statements the situation is quite different. To know the meaning of the evaluative expressions is not by itself sufficient for knowing under what conditions the statements containing them are true or false, because the meaning of the expressions is such that the statements are not capable of objective or factual truth or falsity at all. Any justification a speaker can give for one of his evaluative statements essentially involves some appeal to attitudes he holds, to criteria of assessment he has adopted, or to moral principles by which he has chosen to live and judge other people. Descriptive statements are thus objective, evaluative statements subjective, and the difference is a consequence of the different sorts of terms employed.

The underlying reason for these differences is that evaluative statements perform a completely different job from descriptive statements. Their job is not to describe any features of the world but to express the speaker's emotions, to express his attitudes, to praise or condemn, to laud or insult, to commend, to recommend, to advise, to command, and so forth. Once we see the different illocutionary forces the two kinds of utterances have, we see that there must be a logical gulf between them. Evaluative statements must be different from descriptive statements in order to do their job, for if they were objective they could no longer function to evaluate. Put metaphysically, values cannot lie in the world, for if they did they would cease to be values and would just be another part of the world. Put in the formal mode, one cannot define an evaluative word in terms of descriptive words, for if one did, one would no longer be able to use the evaluative word to commend, but only to describe. Put yet another way, any effort to derive an "ought" from an "is" must be a waste of time, for all it could show even if it succeeded would be that the "is" was not a real "is" but only a disguised "ought" or, alternatively, that the "ought" was not a real "ought" but only a disguised "is".

This picture engenders a certain model of the way evaluative statements relate to descriptive statements. According to the classical model, an inference from a descriptive statement or statements to an evaluative statement, if valid, must always be mediated by an additional evaluative statement. A rational reconstruction of such arguments has the form:

Evaluative major premise:	e.g., one ought to keep all one's promises;
Descriptive minor premise:	e.g., Jones promised to do X;
Therefore, evaluative conclusion:	Therefore, Jones ought to do X.

It is essential to this model that the criteria for deciding whether a statement is evaluative or descriptive must be independent of these alleged entailment relations. That is, we are supposed to be able to identify independently a class of descriptive statements and a class of evaluative statements about which we then make a *further* and *independent* discovery that members of the former class cannot by themselves entail members of the latter class. If we *define* "evaluative" and "descriptive" so that the thesis holds, it becomes completely trivial. I mention this point because in these disputes the person who holds that descriptive statements cannot entail evaluative statements is often tempted to trivialize his position by invoking the classical model in such a trivialized fashion. To his opponent he says: "You claim that these descriptive statements entail these evaluative statements, but that only shows that these apparently descriptive statements cannot be really descriptive or that these apparently evaluative statements cannot be really evaluative." Such a reply is an admission of defeat.

The point of my counter-example is to show that the classical model is incapable of dealing with institutional facts. It is often a matter of fact that one has certain obligations, commitments, rights, and responsibilities, but it is a matter of institutional, not brute, fact. It is one such institutionalized form of obligation, promising, which I invoked above to derive an "ought" from an "is". I started with a brute fact, that a man uttered certain words, and then invoked the institution in such a way as to generate institutional facts by which we arrived at the conclusion that, as regards his obligation, the man ought to pay another man five dollars. The whole proof rests on an appeal to the constitutive rule that to make a promise is to undertake an obligation, and this rule is a meaning rule of the 'descriptive' word "promise". For the old: "No set of descriptive statements can entail an evaluative conclusion without the addition of at least one evaluative premise", we could substitute: "No set of brute fact statements can entail an institutional fact statement without the addition of at least one constitutive rule." I do not know for sure that this last is true, but I am inclined to think it is, and it is at least consistent with the facts of the above derivation.

We are now in a position to see how we can generate an indefinite number of such proofs. Consider the following vastly different example. We are in our half of the seventh inning and I have a big lead off second base. The pitcher whirls, fires to the shortstop covering, and I am tagged out a good ten feet down the line. The umpire shouts, "Out!" I, however, being a positivist, hold my ground. The umpire tells me to return to the dugout. I point out to him that you can't derive an "ought" from an "is". No set of descriptive statements describing matters of fact, I say, will entail any evaluative statements to the effect that I should or ought to leave the field. "You just can't get evaluations from facts alone. What is needed is an evaluative major premise." I therefore return to and stay on second base (until no doubt I am shortly carried off the field). I think everyone feels my claims here to be preposterous, and preposterous in the sense of logically absurd. Of course you can derive an "ought" from an "is", and though to actually set out the derivation in this case would be more complicated than in the case of promising, it is, in principle, no different. By undertaking to play baseball I have committed myself to the observance of certain constitutive rules.

We are now also in a position to see that the tautology that one ought to keep one's promises is only one of a class of similar tautologies concerning institutionalized forms of obligation.

For example, "One ought not to steal" can be (though of course it need not be) taken as saying that to recognize something as someone else's property necessarily involves recognizing that he has a right to dispose of it. This is a constitutive rule of the institution of private property.[1] "One ought not to tell lies" can be taken as saying that to make an assertion necessarily involves undertaking an obligation to speak truthfully. Another constitutive rule. "One ought to pay one's debts" can be construed as saying that to recognize something as a debt is necessarily to recognize an obligation to pay it. Of course, to repeat, there are other ways to construe these sentences which would not render the proposition expressed in their utterance a tautology. It is easy to see how all these principles will generate counter-examples to the thesis that you cannot derive an "ought" from an "is".

My tentative conclusions, then, are as follows:

1. The classical picture fails to account for institutional facts.
2. Institutional facts exist within systems of constitutive rules.
3. Some systems of constitutive rules involve obligations, commitments, and responsibilities.
4. Within some of those systems we can derive "ought's" from "is's" on the model of the first derivation.

With these conclusions we now return to the question with which I began this section: How can my stating a fact about a man, such as the fact that he made a promise, commit me to a view about what he ought to do? One can begin to answer this question by saying that for me to state such an institutional fact is already to invoke the constitutive rules of the institution. It is those rules that give the word "promise" its meaning. But those rules are such that to commit myself to the view that Jones made a promise involves committing myself to what he ought to do, at

[1] Proudhon said: "property is theft". If one tries to take this as an internal remark it makes no sense. It was intended as an external remark attacking and rejecting the institution of private property. It gets its air of paradox and its force by using terms which are internal to the institution in order to attack the institution.

Standing on the deck of some institutions one can tinker with constitutive rules and even throw some other institutions overboard. But could one throw all institutions overboard (in order perhaps to avoid ever having to derive an "ought" from an "is")? One could not and still engage in those forms of behavior we consider characteristically human. Suppose Proudhon had added (and tried to live by): "Truth is a lie, marriage is infidelity, language is uncommunicative, law is a crime", and so on with every possible institution.

least as regards the obligation he undertook in promising. If you like then, we have shown that "promise" is an evaluative word since we have shown that the notion of promising is logically tied to the evaluative notion of obligation, but since it also is purely 'descriptive' (because it is a matter of objective fact whether or not someone made a promise), we have really shown that the whole distinction needs to be re-examined. The alleged distinction between descriptive and evaluative statements is really a conflation of at least two distinctions. On the one hand there is a distinction between different kinds of illocutionary acts, one family of illocutionary acts including evaluations, another family including descriptions. On the other hand there is a distinction between utterances which involve claims objectively decidable as true or false and those which involve claims not objectively decidable, but which are 'matters of personal decision' or 'matters of opinion'. It has been assumed that the former distinction is (must be) a special case of the latter, that if something has the illocutionary force of an evaluation, it cannot be entailed by factual premises. If I am right, then the alleged distinction between descriptive and evaluative utterances is useful only as a distinction between two kinds of illocutionary force, describing and evaluating, and it is not even very useful there since, if we are to use these terms strictly, they are only two among hundreds of kinds of illocutionary forces; and utterances of sentences of the form 5—"Jones ought to pay Smith five dollars"—would not characteristically fall in either class.

What bearing does all this have on moral philosophy? At least this much: It is often claimed that no ethical statement can ever follow from a set of statements of fact. The reason for this, it is alleged, is that ethical statements are a sub-class of evaluative statements, and no evaluative statement can ever follow from a set of statements of fact. The naturalistic fallacy as applied to ethics is just a special case of the general naturalistic fallacy. I have argued that the general claim that one cannot derive evaluative from descriptive statements is false. I have not argued, or even considered, the special claim that specifically ethical or moral statements cannot be derived from statements of fact. However, it does follow from my account that if the special claim is to be demonstrated, it will have to be demonstrated on some independent grounds and cannot be demonstrated on the basis of the general claim since, if my analysis is correct, the general claim is false.

I think, incidentally, that the obligation to keep a promise probably has no necessary connection with morality. It is often claimed that the obligation to keep a promise is a paradigm case of a moral obligation. But consider the following very common sort of example. I promise to come to your party. On the night in question, however, I just don't feel like going. Of course I *ought* to go, after all, I promised and I have no good excuse for not going. But I just don't go. Am I *immoral*? Remiss, no doubt. If it were somehow very important that I go, then it might be immoral of me to stay home. But then the immorality would derive from the importance of my going, and not simply from the obligation undertaken in promising.

8.3 *Objections and replies*

The reader unfamiliar with the philosophical controversy surrounding this problem may well feel that the claims made in section 8.1 are harmless and obvious enough. Yet there is no contention in this book that will arouse and has aroused as much controversy as the derivation in that section. Published criticisms of the derivation tend to fall into two categories—those which attacked the *ceteris paribus* clause and those which attacked the alleged logical connection between promising, obligation, and "ought". The first set I have sidestepped by excluding from consideration within the proof the various kinds of consideration that the *ceteris paribus* clause is designed to deal with. The second set goes to the heart of the matter at issue and deserves consideration in more detail. These objections to the derivation are very revealing of many problems, both in the philosophy of language and elsewhere. In what follows I shall present and answer in dialogue form what I take to be the most sincere objections made against the proof.

First objection: There is a kind of conservatism implicit in the whole account. You seem to be saying that it is logically inconsistent for anyone to think that one ought never to keep promises, or that the whole institution of promising is evil.

Reply: This objection really is a misunderstanding of the whole proof and, in fact, a misunderstanding of the whole book. It is perfectly consistent with my account for someone to argue "One ought never to keep promises". Suppose for example a nihilistic anarchist argues that one ought never to keep promises because, e.g., an unseemly concern with obligation impedes self-fulfillment. Such an argument may be silly, but it is not, as far as my account is concerned, logically absurd. To understand this point, we need to make a distinction between what is external and what is internal to the institution of promising. It is internal to the concept of promising that in promising one undertakes an obligation to do something. But whether the entire institution of promising is good or evil, and whether the obligations undertaken in promising are overridden by other outside considerations are questions which are external to the institution itself. The nihilist argument considered above is simply an external attack on the institution of promising. In effect, it says that the obligation to keep a promise is always overridden because of the alleged evil character of the institution. But it does not deny the point that promises obligate, it only insists that the obligations ought not to be fulfilled because of the external consideration of "self-fulfillment"

Nothing in my account commits one to the conservative view that institutions are logically unassailable or to the view that one ought to approve or disapprove this or that institution. The point is merely that when one enters an institutional activity by invoking the rules of the institution one necessarily commits oneself in such and such ways, regardless of whether one approves or disapproves of the institution. In the case of linguistic institutions, like promising (or statement making), the serious utterances of the words commit one in ways which are determined by the meaning of the words. In certain first-person utterances, the utterance is the undertaking of an obligation. In certain third-person utterances, the utterance is a report of an obligation undertaken.

Second objection: The answer to the first objection suggests the following *reductio ad absurdum*. On this account, any institution could arbitrarily obligate anyone depending only on how one arbitrarily decides to set up the institution.

Reply: This objection is based on an incorrect conception of obligations which is not implied by the account given here. The notion of an obligation is closely tied to the notion of accepting, acknowledging, recognizing, undertaking, etc., obligations in such a way as to render the notion of an obligation essentially a contractual notion.[1] Suppose a group of people in Australia completely unknown to me sets up a 'rule' whereby I am 'obligated'

[1] Cf. E. J. Lemmon, 'Moral Dilemmas', *Philosophical Review* (1962).

to pay them $100 a week. Unless I am somehow involved in the original agreement, their claims are unintelligible. Not just any arbitrary decision by X can place Y under an obligation.

Third objection: But now it begins to emerge that the original evaluative decision is the decision to accept or reject the institution of promising. On your account as soon as someone uses the word "promise" seriously he is committed in such and such ways, which only shows that the evaluative premise is $1a$. It shows that $1a$ is really a substantial moral principle.

Reply: This objection begins to approach the heart of the matter. $1a$ is indeed a crucial premise, for it is the one which gets us from the brute to the institutional level, the level that contains obligations. But its 'acceptance' is quite unlike the decision to accept a certain moral principle. $1a$ states a fact about the meaning of a descriptive word, "promise". Furthermore, anyone who uses that word in serious literal speech is committed to its logical consequences involving obligations. And there is nothing special in this respect about promises; similar rules are built into statements, warnings, advice, reports, perhaps even commands. I am here challenging a certain model of describing linguistic facts. According to that model, once you have described the facts in any situation, the question of any 'evaluations' is still left absolutely open. What I am here arguing is that, in the case of certain institutional facts, the evaluations involving obligations, commitments, and responsibilities are no longer left completely open because the statement of the institutional facts involves these notions.

It is a matter of immense fascination to me that authors who are "anti-naturalists" when they think about it, tacitly accept the derivations of evaluative from descriptive when they are just doing philosophy and disregarding their ideology. Consider the following passages from R. M. Hare:[1] "If a person says that a thing is red, he is *committed* [my italics] to the view that anything which was like it in the relevant respects would likewise be red." Hare also says[2] that he is committed "*to calling it red*" [my italics]; and this is purely in virtue of the meaning of the relevant words. Leaving aside the question of whether what Hare says is true,[3] it is of the same form as my argument. I say if a person promises

---

[1] R. M. Hare, *Freedom and Reason* (Oxford, 1963), p. 11.   [2] *Ibid.* p. 15.
[3] It can't be quite true in its stronger version on p. 15. A man may call one object red and not say anything at all about the next red object he sees.

he is committed to doing the thing promised, and this is purely in virtue of the meaning of "promise".

The only important difference between the two theses is that the commitment in Hare's example is to future linguistic behaviour. The commitment in mine is not restricted to linguistic behaviour. In structure, they are identical. But let us suppose someone can show they are not the same; very well, then I should simply conduct my derivation on this example. "He called it red" is a straightforward statement of fact (like, e.g., "he promised"). "He is committed to perform a certain act" is evaluative since commitment (though wider than) is a member of the same family as obligation. Hence it is the very thesis of Hare's example that evaluative statements follow from descriptive statements. Hare is disturbed by what he takes to be the claim that tautologies generate obligations.[1] But what he appears to overlook is that the tautologies are hypothetical and hence do not by themselves generate any obligations. What they say is e.g. "If he calls it red, he is committed". So we need the empirical premise, "He called it red" to get the conclusion: "He is committed." No one is claiming that tautologies 'prescribe' behaviour categorically but only conditionally on some institutional fact (as Hare's example illustrates).

In reply to this point, it might be said that all he meant by "committed" is that a speaker who did not observe these comitments would be contradicting himself. Thus, commitments are construed 'descriptively'. But this only forces the question back a step. Why should a speaker concern himself at all if his statements are self-contradictory? And the answer is clearly that it is internal to the notion of a statement (descriptive word) that a self-contradiction (descriptive word) is a defect (evaluative word). That is, he who states is committed (*ceteris paribus*) to avoiding self-contradictions. One does not first decide to make statements and then make a separate evaluative decision that they would be better if they were not self-contradictory. So we are still left with commitments being essentially involved in facts.

Fourth objection: The answer to the third objection really misses the point. All you have shown in your derivation is that "promise" (and no doubt "state", "describe" and certain others) are really evaluative words. It may be useful to point out that notions we once thought descriptive are really evaluative, but that

---

[1] 'The promising game', *Revue Internationale de Philosophie* (1964), pp. 403 ff.

in no way gets over the descriptive–evaluative gap. Having shown that 2 is evaluative, all that really follows is that 1*a* must be evaluative since the descriptive premises 1 and 1*b* are insufficient to entail 2 by themselves.

Reply: There is no independent motivation for calling 2 evaluative, other than the fact that it entails an evaluative statement 3. So now the thesis that descriptions cannot entail evaluations is becoming trivial, for the criterion of whether or not a statement is descriptive will be whether or not it entails something evaluative. But unless there are independently identifiable classes of descriptive and evaluative statements about which we can then further discover that members of the former do or do not entail members of the latter, our definition of descriptive will include "does not entail any evaluative statements", and that will render our thesis trivial. 2 is intuitively a straightforward statement of fact. If our linguistic theory forces us to deny that, and to assert that it is a subjective evaluation, then there is something wrong with the theory.

Fifth objection: The fourth objection needs merely to be restated. The point about words like "promise" is that they have both an evaluative and a descriptive sense. In the descriptive sense (sense 1) "promise" means simply *uttering certain words*. In the evaluative sense (sense 2) "promise" means *undertaking an obligation*. Now, if 1*a* really is descriptive, then all your move from 1 to 2 proves is that Jones made a promise in sense 1, but in order to get from 2 to 3 you would have to prove he made a promise in sense 2 and that would require an extra evaluative premise.

In short, there is a simple fallacy of equivocation over "promise". You prove that Jones made a promise in sense 1 and then assume that you have proved he made a promise in sense 2 by assuming incorrectly that these two senses are the same. The difference between sense 2 and sense 1 is the difference between a committed participant and a neutral observer. It is both necessary and decisive to make this distinction between the committed participant and the neutral observer, for it is only the neutral observer who is making genuine factual or descriptive statements. As soon as you interpret the word "promise" from the point of view of the committed participant you have tacitly slipped in an evaluation but, until you have done that, the proof will not work. You really should not suppose that every word comes already marked as evaluative or descriptive. Some apparently descriptive words can have an evaluative sense, as in sense 2 of "promise", as well as a descriptive sense. It is only in sense 1 of "promise" that it is purely descriptive.

Reply: There is no sense 1. That is, there is no literal meaning of "promise" in which all it means is uttering certain words. Rather "promise" denotes speech acts characteristically performed in the utterance of certain words. But "promise" is not lexically ambiguous as between uttering words and undertaking obligations. The objection above tries to offer a sense of promise in which the statement "He made a promise" would state a brute fact and not an institutional fact, but there is no such sense. The reasoning in this objection is the same as in objection 4. It consists of the invocation of the classical model, but it is precisely the classical model that is here being challenged.

I shall try to spell this out a bit more. Linguistic facts as stated in linguistic characterizations provide the constraints on any linguistic theory. At a minimum, the theory must be consistent with the facts; an acceptable theory would also have to account for or explain the facts. Now in the present instance the following linguistic characterizations state certain facts:

1. A statement of the form "X made a promise" states an objective fact and, except in borderline cases, is not subjective or a matter of opinion.

2. By definition, promising is undertaking an obligation or commitment, etc., to do something.

3. A sentence of the form "X made a promise" is not lexically ambiguous as between "X said some words" and "X really promised". "Promise" is not thus homonymous.

4. Promising is characteristically performed by uttering certain sorts of expressions in certain contexts and with certain intentions.

5. A statement of the form "X undertook an obligation" is 'evaluative', since it is a statement predicating the so-called evaluative notion, obligation.

Consistency with these facts is a condition of adequacy on any linguistic theory purporting to deal with this area. Objection 4 is inconsistent with statement 1. Objection 5 patches up that point by being inconsistent with statement 3. Both of these maneuvers are motivated by the failure of the classical model to account for 1 and 2 together, given 5. Nearly all of the objections to the proof consist of efforts to deny one or more of these linguistic characterizations.

The objection you just made (5) is an attempt to introduce a sense of "promise" in which a promise is not an undertaking, but is completely defined in terms of statement 4. But there is no such literal sense. You are motivated to that maneuver because your theory cannot accommodate both the fact that promises obligate and the fact that it *is* a matter of fact that someone has made a promise.

Sixth objection: Well, I am still not convinced so let me try again. It seems to me you do not adequately appreciate my distinction between the committed participant and the neutral observer. Now I can agree with you that as soon as we literally and unreservedly use the word "promise", an evaluative element enters in, for by literally and unreservedly using that word we are committing ourselves to the institution of promising. But that involves an evaluation, so as soon as you specify which of the early uses is a literal and committed use we can see that it is really evaluative.

Reply: In a way, you are here stating my argument as if it were an objection against me. When we do use a word literally and unreservedly we are indeed committing ourselves to the logical properties of that word. In the case of promise, when we assert "He made a promise" we commit ourself to the proposition that he undertook an obligation. In exactly the same way, when we use the word "triangle" we commit ourselves to its logical properties. So that when we say, e.g., "X is a triangle" we commit ourselves to the proposition that X has three sides. And the fact that the commitment in the first case involves the notion of obligation shows that we are able to derive from it an 'evaluative' conclusion, but it does not show that there is anything subjective (matter of opinion, not a matter of fact, or a matter of moral decision) in the statement "He made a promise", any more than the fact that the statement "X is a triangle" has logical consequences, shows that there is a moral decision involved in the committed use of the word "triangle".

I think the reason you are confused here is simply this. There are two radically different ways of taking the phrase "commit oneself to (accept) the institution of promising". In one way it means something like (*a*) "undertake to use the word "promise" in accordance with its literal meaning, which literal meaning is determined by the internal constitutive rules of the institution". A quite different way to take the phrase is to take it as meaning (*b*) "endorse the institution as a good or acceptable institution". Now, when I do assert literally that he made a promise I do indeed commit myself to the institution in the sense of (*a*); indeed, it is precisely because the literal meaning involves me in this commitment that the derivation goes through. But I do not commit myself in the sense of (*b*). It is perfectly possible for someone who loathes the institution of promising to say quite literally, " Jones made a promise", thus committing himself to the view that Jones undertook an obligation. Sense (*b*) of commitment really is a matter of opinion (at least as far as the present discussion is concerned) but there is nothing subjective about the statements made involving commitments in the sense of interpretation (*a*). To make this clear, note that exactly the same distinction holds for geometry. Someone who thinks the whole study and subject of geometry is evil still commits himself to the logical consequences of "*X* is a triangle" when he asserts "*X* is a triangle". In neither case is there anything evaluative—in the sense of subjectiveness—about the commitment. Both "He made a promise" and "*X* is a triangle" are statements of fact. (Of course it is logically possible for people to try to sabotage promising—or geometry—by using words in incoherent ways, but that is irrelevant to the validity of the derivations in both cases.)

Now, when you say that the evaluative element enters in when we literally and unreservedly characterize something as a promise, that can mean one of two things, either:

1. The statement "He made a promise" made literally and unreservedly entails the evaluative statement "He undertook an obligation"; or

2. The statement "He made a promise" is always subjective or a matter of opinion because to make it involves thinking that the institution of promising is a good thing.

Now in the first case, what you say is quite true and indeed is the crux of my argument and rests on interpretation (*a*) above. But if what you mean is expressed by the second claim, which is based on interpretation (*b*), then it is obviously false. It is obviously false both that "He made a promise" is subjective or a matter of opinion and false that in order to say unreservedly, "He made a promise" one needs to think the institution of promising a good thing.

In the classical theory of 'evaluative' statements, there are two elements, one, the recognition of a class of statements intuitively felt to be evaluative (unfortunately it turns out that this is a very heterogeneous class indeed) and secondly, the theory that all such statements must be subjective or a matter of opinion. I am not challenging the first half of this; I think there are certain paradigms at least of evaluative utterances, and I am willing to go along with the orthodox theorists that "He is under an obligation" is one of them. But what I am challenging is the second half, the theory that every member of this class must be subjective and that no factual or objective statement can entail any member of this class.

Seventh objection: I am still unconvinced. Why can't I speak in a detached anthropological sense? It seems obvious to me that one can say "He made a promise", meaning something like "He made what they, the people of this Anglo-Saxon tribe, call a promise". And that is a purely descriptive sense of promise which involves no commitment to evaluative statements at all. Now it is this anthropological point of view that I am trying to express when I make my distinction between the committed participant and the neutral observer.

Reply: Of course, you can speak in *oratio obliqua*, and thus avoid the commitments of speaking straight out. You can even employ the forms of speech for speaking normally and still be speaking in disguised *oratio obliqua*, or what you called the detached anthropological sense. But notice that this is really quite irrelevant and does not show that there are different senses of the words involved, or that the original statement was a concealed evaluation. For notice that one can do exactly the same thing with any word you like. One can adopt a detached anthropological attitude toward geometry, and indeed a skeptical anthropologist from another planet might adopt just such an attitude.[1] When he says "X is a triangle" he might mean no more than "X is what they, the Anglo-Saxons, call a triangle", but that doesn't show that there are two senses of "triangle", a committed or evaluative sense and a detached or

---

[1] Notice incidentally that anthropologists do in fact talk about religions in this way: e.g. "there are two gods, of whom the rain god is the more important for it is he who produces rain". This does not show that there are different meanings to any words involved, it merely shows that it is possible in certain contexts to speak in *oratio obliqua* without employing the forms of *oratio obliqua*.

descriptive sense. Nor does it show that Euclid was a disguised moralist because his proofs require a 'committed' use of the terms involved. The fact that one can adopt a detached attitude toward anything at all is irrelevant to the validity of deductive arguments involving the committed use of the words involved. If it were really a valid objection to the derivation in section 8.1 to say that by reinterpreting the words in a detached anthropological sense we can produce an invalid argument, then the same objection would refute every possible deductive argument, because every valid argument depends on the committed occurrence of the terms crucial to the derivation. All the objection says is that for any deductive argument whatever you can construct a parallel argument in *oratio obliqua* from which the conclusion of the original cannot be validly derived. But so what? Such a fact could never affect the validity of any of the original arguments. What my argument requires, like any valid argument, is a serious, literal, non-*oratio obliqua* occurrence of the crucial words it contains. The fact that there are other possible non-serious occurrences of these words is quite irrelevant.

Of all the arguments used against the original proof, the argument from anthropology is both the most common[1] and the weakest. It has the following structure: Take any valid derivation of a conclusion from premises. Then take any crucial word *W* in the premises, be it "promise", "triangle", "red", any word you like which is crucial to the argument. Reinterpret *W* so it doesn't mean *W* but means, e.g. "what somebody else calls *W*". Now rewrite the derivation with *W* so reinterpreted and see if it is still valid. Chances are it is not; but, if it is, keep repeating the same procedure with other words until you get a version where it is not. Conclusion: the derivation was invalid all along.

The fact that the critics of the derivation repeatedly advance an argument which, if it were valid, would threaten all valid derivations is illustrative of the irony I cited at the beginning of this chapter. The urge to read the metaphysical distinction between Fact and Value back into language as a thesis about valid entailment relations must inevitably run up against counter-examples, because speaking a language is everywhere permeated with the facts of commitments undertaken, obligations assumed, cogent

---

[1] In spite of the fact that it was considered and answered in the original presentation. Cf. J. R. Searle, *op. cit.* pp. 51 and 52.

arguments presented, and so on. In the face of these counter-examples the temptation becomes overwhelming to reconstrue the terminology of the counter-examples in a 'descriptive' vein, to adopt the 'detached anthropological standpoint'. But the price of doing that is that words no longer mean what they mean and the price of a really consistent application of the 'detached anthropological standpoint' would be an end to all validity and entailment. The attempt to elude the counter-examples and repair the inconsistency by retreating from the committed use of the words is motivated by the desire to cling to the thesis, come what may. But the retreat from the committed use of words ultimately must involve a retreat from language itself, for speaking a language—as has been the main theme of this book— consists of performing speech acts according to rules, and there is no separating those speech acts from the commitments which form essential parts of them.

INDEX

Index

Index